JULIAN'S CHALLENGE

JULIAN'S CHALLENGE

Robert H. Calderwood

VANTAGE PRESS
New York

Scriptural references are from the New Revised Standard Version (NRSV).

Published by Vantage Press, Inc.
516 West 34th Street, New York, New York 10001

Manufactured in the United States of America
ISBN: 0-533-11143-9

Library of Congress Catalog Card No.: 94-90235

0 9 8 7 6 5 4 3 2 1

To The Most Reverend Edwin Lackey, Bishop of Ottawa (1971–93), during which time he was also the Metropolitan of the Ecclesiastical Province of Ontario; in thanksgiving for his life and witness in the Christian faith, and for the pleasure of having him as a friend.

As truly as God is our Father, so just as truly is God our Mother.

In our Father, God Almighty, we have our being; in our merciful Mother we are remade and restored.

Our fragmented lives are knit together.

And by giving and yielding ourselves, through grace, to the Holy Spirit, we are made whole.

It is I, the strength and goodness of the Fatherhood.

It is I, the wisdom of the Motherhood.

It is I, the light and grace of holy love.

It is I, the Trinity, it is I, the unity.

I am the sovereign goodness of all things.

It is I who teach you to love.

It is I who teach you to desire.

It is I who am the reward of all true desiring.

All shall be well, and all shall be well, and all manner of thing shall be well.

—Julian of Norwich

Contents

Acknowledgments

First and foremost, it is a privilege to express my sincerest gratitude to Judith Lackey. By her gracious consent, I have dedicated this work to The Most Reverend Edwin Lackey. There were many occasions on which the Archbishop and I met for lunch since I returned to my home diocese in 1989; he and I renewed our friendship and shared many of our joys and concerns about the place of the Church in our society. At one particular luncheon, I mentioned that I had been doing considerable research on Julian of Norwich and that I was at the point of producing a manuscript. A joyous expression came to his face, and he exclaimed his long-time interest in this lady. He made me promise that I would let him read the finished product. He never did. Thus, I am privileged to be allowed to make this dedication to my friend and bishop.

Second, my heartfelt appreciation for and my profound gratitude to many people who encouraged me, guided me, and suffered with me to bring to publication this look at Julian of Norwich.

Introduction: The Challenge

Julian challenges me. She has forced a wrestling in my mind that I tried to ignore. The more it was ignored, the stronger that challenge was experienced. Humankind has wrestled since creation concerning the knowledge acquired about God. That knowledge is still of vital importance for human beings to discover who She/He is. The reading of Julian has caused me to rethink theological concepts where theological phrases discovered and learned made me suppose that I had caught the reality about God. But there is a danger in such glibness, for many of us have too easily accepted phrases, names, and concepts for the Creator. In fact, so glib has been the acceptance that we more readily declared the meaning without wrestling with what is the message in those concepts and phrases and what is being related to the general populace. There just may be more understanding to be discovered about God. Many people, for example, see in the word *God* the actuality of "hope" and "life." Others will argue "Is He fate or Father?" There is a sense that others know His name ultimately. It is God-Father, Father of Jesus. To have such a sense may well have been born from an acquired knowledge and may well have been undergirded with joy and trust, but such a sense does not come only or at all through acquired theological phraseology. It comes from a sense of experiencing the Creator in creation, which allows another to say that they know Her name ultimately. It is God-Mother; Mother of Nurture, Compassion, and Wisdom. I accept the challenge from Julian to wrestle and to discover a fuller understanding of the Creator-God-Mother. Jacob never received a complete answer from his wrestling—who God is (Gen. 32:22–30). Through Julian's message, I hope a rich discovery about the nature of God will become a part of reality for me and the reader.

Julian challenges me a second time. She gives a new dimension to Wisdom. Early in the longer version, recording her revelations, Julian shares her experiences of Wisdom as a divine person. Fiorenza states quite well that which Julian could easily accept: "Wisdom sought a dwelling place among humanity, but found none."[1] Julian attempts to call all humankind to a rediscovery of the Sophia-God. The divine Sophia is the God of the ancient Jewish tribes. Throughout Wisdom books and other scriptural passages, "Sophia" is sister, mother, beloved, teacher. She is the leader, the preacher. As we hear of Jesus, so we hear of Sophia searching out people, inviting them into the security of a home, offering rest, knowledge, life. It is Sophia who makes all things well (Wisdom 7:24, 27). The challenge here is to discover all the treasures of wisdom; it is not that one of the treasures is necessarily female or simply another attribute of the Trinity, but it is to discover Her to be more a part of us than we ever believed. If Sophia is my sister, mother, beloved, teacher, this gives a different and deeper meaning to Matthew 12:50,[2] so much so that past interpretation has not captured the Mother-God essence in the nature of the Godhead, but has allowed only the understanding that fits well into patriarchal, androcentric, legalistic, and judgemental mould.

Julian offers me a third and, perhaps, last challenge. It is not that the Creator is masculine or feminine because that has such a finite quality; but that the Creator has the very essence and reality of the masculine and the feminine is most significant. Once this concept is acceptable, then the Essence is believed to be mutually interdependent; and if that is real, then so must the creation itself be mutually interdependent. Our inherited attitudes then are no longer relevant if the Church and the community are to accomplish their task. Old isolations must go and new relationships must be born and nurtured. Relationships will spring from a deeper and richer understanding of what equality, mutual responsibility, interdependence, and creation mean.

If Julian's challenges fail to be wrestled with, and if we think these merely mean a change of language, then the Church and the community have lost insight and the preciousness of a simple yet profound spirituality that will remain in Julian's century. A great freedom will have disappeared. To prevent such a disappearance is to pay the price for that freedom. In this late twentieth-century world, that price is the voluntary acceptance of each of a complete sharing in each other's tasks and the acknowledgement of each other's individuality. This third challenge dares us to find the freedom and the interdependence and at the same time to rejoice in the discovery; the challenge dares us to discover further that interdependence and mutuality are not new concepts or images; they are imbedded deeply in the teaching of Scripture about the nature of the Creator and humankind.

Notes

1. Elisabeth Schussler Fiorenza, *In Memory of Her* (New York: Crossroad Publishing, 1990) 133.
2. The Matthew reference reads: "For whoever does the will of my Father in heaven is my brother and sister and mother."

JULIAN'S CHALLENGE

1

The Lady: Julian of Norwich

We know very little about Julian's life. We do not even know her real name. History calls her Julian of Norwich because the name of the local parish church that she attended was named Julian.

Julian was born in Norwich, circa 1342. Norwich was a thriving, bustling city, and Julian's spirituality was born and nourished in the middle of it. Historians speculate regarding her education, although by her own admission she was unlettered. What that actually means draws several contradictory conclusions from various sources.[1] Some contend she was uneducated, while others claim she received learning from the Benedictine convent at Carrow.[2]

Her writing style betrays any claim that she would be uneducated. Julian mastered literary skills better than most of her contemporaries. Besides being competent in English, there is evidence that she had at least a working knowledge of French. The most cryptic view of her writings shows that many ideas that were current on the European continent are in her presentations; consequently, she not only had access to foreign manuscripts but also was able to read them.

Too, she probably belonged to the merchant class, if not the upper class, whose members had access to higher learning at such institutions as Oxford. Historical accounts reveal that specific "courses" were offered in disciplines similar to those on the curriculum of our community colleges today.

One further comment reveals the continued speculation about Julian's education. The possibility of her having received an education in a university could be a modern extrapolation of the manner in which one receives an education in the twentieth century. It is undisputed that women in the Middle Ages were commonly educated in convents, some of which had a very solid reputation for scholarship. Generally, women were not accepted in universities in either England or France; there are dubious citings of Italian women at Bologna University. On the other hand, there is little doubt that other women were tutored or schooled individually by clerics, the education of Heloise being a prime example. As previously stated, Julian was well-versed in European scholastic achievements, which could suggest that if she did not receive her education on the continent, certainly she was a student, par excellence, of a notable scholar cleric.

I must leave the discussion of Julian's education at this point. Although I am too willing to allow that she obtained an education equal to a university level, I must succumb to the more documented evaluation. The only real legitimate argument is the historical guess that for her time and place, the woman Julian, through a well-learned cleric tutor, achieved her status of education at a convent.

Julian lived to an age beyond the normal life expectancy of her time. She died circa 1417, some seventy-five years after her birth, a remarkable age when we consider that England experienced more than one outbreak of the bubonic plague during the years 1342 to 1417. Had she been a traveller, Julian would have witnessed tumultuous times in England and Europe, disharmony within the Church, the Avignon papacy, the Great Schism, parts of the One Hundred Years' War, the Peasant Revolt, civil war, and the deposing of Richard the II, to mention a few misfortunes.[3]

Speculation also surrounds Julian's life as a nun. Some argue that she became a Benedictine at Carrow. In actual fact, we do not know. Doubt too exists concerning social status during the time of her "revelations"; it would seem that the "showings" are the experiences of a deeply religious woman still living at home. It was during the time that she was writing the longer version of her experiences that we can say with any certainty that she was an anchoress.

The solitary vocation of an anchoress was not unusual in the medieval era. Around Norwich there were over fifty "cells" between the time of Julian's birth in the fourteenth century to the Reformation in the sixteenth century. To become an anchoress, Julian would have had to receive the permission and support of her bishop. Potential solitaries would have needed to prove that they were responding to a genuine call of God and that they had an adequate means of support. A special Mass would be celebrated, and the new anchoress would be taken to her anchorhold or cell. This cell was a small room usually built into the Cathedral or chapel wall. There the person would live the rest of her life.

An anchoress such as Julian was a hermit. Withdrawing from society, she devoted her life completely to meditation and prayer; in Julian's case committing to writing her "relevations" and expounding what she held to be true from these about the nature of God and of Jesus Christ was an additional task. In her cell, there was a small opening or window through which she could see the Mass being celebrated and receive Communion. Too, as many people came to seek counsel, she was able to communicate with the populace through this window.

Counselling was an important part of the life of the anchoress or hermit. While free from the hustle of mercantile transactions, she could not forget or ignore its existence. Through the window of the anchorhold, Julian gave counsel. She listened to the woes of society, prescribed remedies, offered consultations, and shared her experiences of God's love, which she gained through her "revelations" or "showings."

After her religious experiences from God, she wrote a short version of these happenings; later, some say as much as twenty years later, she authored an extended version of the sixteen showings, which were reported in eighty-six chapters. The subject matter of these showings concerned the Trinity, the sacrifice of the Christ, Jesus/ God as Mother, and the Sophia (Wisdom) of God. It is in the longer text that she translates her experiences (the symbols, images, and parables) into theological concepts.

Julian is claimed as the first Englishwoman and the first theologian to write originally in Chaucerian English. I am learning what others have already discovered, that she is a brilliant scholar, theologian, and spiritualist. Yet Julian was not realistic; she was well aware that her England was suspect, unkind, and disrespectful to any woman who purported to have a strong faith, gifts of counselling, and profound spiritual magnitude. She protested against this treatment in chapter six of her shorter version:

Botte I wate wele, this that I saye, I hafe it of the schewynge of hym that es souerayne techare. Botte sothelye

4

chartye styrres me to telle zowe it, for i wolde god ware knawenn and mynn evynn crystene spede, as I wolde be me selfe to the mare hatynge of synne and louynge of god. Botte for I am a woman, schulde I therfore levew that I schulde nouzt telle zowe the goodenes of god, syne that I sawe in the same tyme that is his wille that it be knaween?[4]

Julian simply recorded her showings, prepared by faith and held in faith. It is good to hear that scholars of this century have awarded her great honours; "her book is undoubtedly the most profound and complex of all medieval spiritual writings."[5]

What have we done? We have suppressed the work of Julian; in fact, most of the works by feminine personages, throughout history, have been thrown aside as of little importance. As noted earlier, Julian held no illusions that her work would be proclaimed as a highly significant theological treatise. Within her shorter text, it is obvious that Julian was aware of the dangers of falling under suspicion. She defends her right to speak out on theological matters even though she is a woman. Predecessors of Julian concerning the teachings of God as our Mother (scriptural references, the works of Saint Anselm and Saint Bernard of Clairvaux, and Cistercian theology) have not been enthusiastically promoted in our theological colleges. Apparently it is the subject matter that threatens the traditional doctrinal policies produced by patriarchal systems.

When reviewing the records of social history, we are strongly reminded that women are to be silent (in the church), and that they have a particular place, i.e. to serve their husbands and not to assume leadership roles.

Certainly such social status imposed on women encouraged scholars to conveniently forget the teachings from Norwich.

We can counter this argument. Other women authors are well-known from medieval times; Christiane de Pizan is one of the most prominent. For example, no other medieval woman spoke so unflinchingly for her sex at every social level. Not only was she a staunch supporter of her sex, but a most prolific writer and the only known woman to have earned her living from her writings.[6] However, she accepted the medieval paradigm agreeing that a woman was naturally subject to man.

There's the rub! To declare so forcefully a teaching that proclaims a status for women contrary to acceptable social practice and to give credence to theological ideas that God is our Mother would be political suicide around the time of Julian. A person in support of these "truths" would be considered as questioning and opposing well-established and enshrined doctrines. Little has changed even into this twentieth century.

As recent as 1978, Cardinal Suenens questioned the Church's silence about the Motherhood of God. "Is there not something specifically feminine in our concept of God? What about her motherhood?" Suenens positively answers his own inquiry: "Yes, in one way there is a feminine as well as a masculine element."[7] To make such "shocking" statements was of little political threat for him, but there has been an extremely quiet acknowledgement of the writing by this prince of the Roman Catholic church. The quiet acknowledgements all through the Christian era are evidence that challenges of this kind are unwelcome.

Why does Julian remain relatively unknown? We continue to speculate. There is a theory that Julian's versions were suppressed either to protect her from suspicion of heresy or because both versions were already banned. To promote God as our Mother certainly would have been regarded as heretical. Again, no one authority would consider a study of her work with any thought toward effecting a doctrinal revision; and she was a woman out of her place. The Church was known to overreact to any deviations from traditional teaching. Of course, these include the seeing of visions, supernatural experiences, or "private teachings" all of which form the background to Julian's "showings." There is historical evidence that during Julian's years in Norwich, the Church brutally suppressed what it saw as a threat to the integrity of the faith and to society in general. Accounts show that there were people under suspicion who were burned at the stake not far from the location of her cell.

It may be that in that atmosphere of hysteria, Julian came under scrutiny for several reasons; we are not told about this by Julian herself, or any student of history. This is a conjecture, but such thoughts are consistent with the time in which she lived.

She could have been suspect because of her book's contents, or of her speaking out about spiritual matters to the uneducated laity, or because Julian was a woman and therefore not a theologian, or because she did not have permission to write about "holy things" in the first place. Finally, one simple explanation. During the time of the Reformation in the sixteenth century, copies of her works could have been destroyed along with many of the existing libraries. Why not the *Revelations?* Julian simply was not noticed as one of the many illustrious writers. I maintain that is a sad commentary indeed.

Julian has so much to give to the Church and to society. Now that she is becoming better known, albeit too slowly, the Church must acknowledge this great stan-dard bearer. The Church owes much to Julian for her impressive theological awakening of the nature of God. Society too must come to realize its debt to this good lady of Norwich. We need to shout out praise for a refreshing rationale on the equality for women and give the recogni-tion that should be rightfully awarded to women, which has been ignored for too long a time. In accepting the challenges Julian has given to me by making the follow-ing hypotheses, it is hoped that this becomes one other voice to be added to the many that are shouting out praise today for Julian of Norwich and that continues in a logi-cal sequence a demand for correcting the status in which historical patriarchal and androcentric paradigms have and are continuing to place womankind.

Notes

1. Grace Jantzen, Sheila Upjohn, Edmund Colledge, and James Walsh (works by these scholars are noted elsewhere in this paper) are a few who comment about Julian's level of education.

2. Catherine Jones, Katharina M. Wilson, ed., "The English Mys-tic—Julian of Norwich," in *Medieval Women Writers* (Athens: The University of Georgia Press, 1984) 271.

3. Gloria Durka, *Praying with Julian of Norwich* (Winona, Minn.: St. Mary's Press, Christian Brothers Publications, 1989) 17.

4. Edmund Colledge and James Walsh, editors, *Book of Showings to the Anchoress Julian of Norwich,* vol. 1. (Toronto: Pontifical Insti-tute of Mediaeval Studies, 1978) 222. Translation: I know well this that I say. I have it on the showing of him who is a sovereign teacher and truly charity urgeth me to tell you of it, for I would that God were known and my fellow-Christians helped [as I would be myself], to the more hating of sin and loving of God. Because I am a woman should I therefore believe that I ought not to tell you about the good-ness of God since I saw at the same time that it is his will that it be known?

5. Margaret Wade Labarge, *A Small Sound of the Trumpet* (Lon-don: A Hamish Hamilton Paperback, 1986) 134.

6. Ibid., 235.

7. Leon-Joseph Cardinal Suenens, *Your God? The Oxford Mission 1977* (London: Darton, Longman and Todd, 1978) 36.

2

"Oure Very Moder": The First Challenge

Julian addresses the most basic of religious questions: Who is God? In the record of her "showings," she has exploded all the traditional teachings of God into a fuller and richer understanding. Her gift allows us to explore God in true role of Mother and she helps us to contemplate that deeper reality of Her/His essence, and to review our relationship with God as Mother, as Father. Creation becomes more powerful. Salvation is revealed with greater compassion, and there is provided an atmosphere in which there can exist a stronger hope. We see, with an excitement that falls little short of ecstasy, the action of God to make us His people that has taken place not in a dictatorial fashion or as a mass herding of mindless sheep. Julian is so right to express God so aptly as Mother.

The first allusion to her teaching on the Motherhood of God is found in Revelation 48: 14 in the longer version of her work.[1] She refers to this place many times as Julian begins to set out her teaching that God/Christ is our Mother:

> and thus is Jhesu oure very moder in kynd of oure furst-makyng, and he is oure very moder in grace by takyng

of oure kynde made . . . I vnderstode thre manner of be-
holdynges of motherhed in god. The furst is grounde of
oure kynde makyng, the seconde is takyng of oure kynde,
and ther begynnyth the moderhed of grace, the thurde is
moderhed in werkyng.[2]

But Julian was not the first to expound this female
essence in reference to the nature of God. Several passages of Scripture in both the Old Testament and the New
Testament give beautiful imagery of God as Mother.[3] One
of the earliest scriptural references is found in the Book
of Numbers. Moses grieves to God about the position in
which he thinks God has placed him. He has led an ancient people into exile, and finds he cannot care for them
adequately; their plight is worsening day by day, and so
he blames God. One is staggered by the picture: he is
standing alone in the desert place; a wildly gesturing,
stammering Moses is enraged at God. "I did not conceive
this people. You [God] must carry this child [these people]
and nurse him." In the text there is no question but that
Moses is picturing God as Mother with Her child nurturing, caring for, and protecting Her love. Moses calls God
to nourish, to watch over and raise him up, and to develop
the nature and character of this people. She (God) only
can do these things. He is Mother of the nation.
Further, in the Old Testament, we read about the
life and times of the Isaiah prophets. Isaiah spells out a
concept that God sees Himself as Mother. One could say
that the author of this section in the Book of Isaiah may
be "putting words into God's mouth," but indeed, all versions of Scripture emphasize the authenticity of this passage by its inclusion.
God as Mother was a very powerful image for Isaiah.[4]
In Isaiah 66: 12–14 particularly, the imagery is intended

to the consolation of Israel and to the spiritual satisfaction of the people attained through nourishment from God . . . as one received a mother's comfort. The point here is not talking of babes, but of the mature Israel. The oldsters who have known wounds, sorrows, injustices, oppression turn to Mother for consolation. It is not at all stretching the point to assert that Isaiah's perspective is that of a new Zion—the messianic community. The new nation born or developed out of the care and protection of their Mother.

Turning to the New Testament, it should come as no surprise to find Jesus using these same concepts of God. He would have learned and studied about these at rabbinical school.[5] He does not refute the imagery but gives further credence to such perceptions. It is both beauty and pathos portrayed; he stands over Jerusalem and is found agonizing over the future of this city, weeping regarding its destruction. "Jerusalem, Jerusalem . . . how often would have I desired to gather your children together as a hen gathers her brood under her wings, and you were not willing!" (Matt. 23:37). Some say this is quoted from the wisdom literature of ancient Judaism. All seem to accept the premise that here Jesus personifies God as a woman (Mother) brooding over the well-being of Her children.

More can be said of Mother imagery from other references in Scripture, but such an investigation must be left for another time and for additional expositions. Before we take a view of Saint Bernard of Clairvaux, however, a predecessor of Julian of Norwich, temptation lures me to pursue a quick glimpse at another important issue. Today the prominence of feminine images is being recognized, more and more. Some still do a great dishonour and disservice to motherhood and femininity, while others are more scholarly and sensitive, giving a sincere and empathetic approach to this imagery. In doing so, those presenting them make an attempt to correct any dishonour. Some correction is even found within religious disciplines, although any attempts to be sensitive and to give a fair recognition to that part of creation could well be interpreted as producing a subtle schism, or could well be seen as the harbingers of hazardous heresy. Perhaps that was the fear of our past religious teachers, so they suppressed and even ignored any reference to feminine imagery in the studies of Scripture or religion.

But serious consideration is to be given to Mother-God images in Scripture, especially when one studies Old Testament writings. Old Testament imagery concerning the womb demands that the womb be revered as "a sign of divine compassion." The Hebrew word *compassion* is consistently rendered "create," "gratifies," "forgives." What is more significant to this translation is that such attributes are believed as to be seen only through the eyes, the wisdom, and the experience of motherhood; and further, that gratuitous kindness in Hebraic history is considered to be unleashed in society through a daughter, a woman, a mother. This is not to suppress fatherly love in such a manner as to enter the equal devastation of making a superior matriarchal society, but it succesfully shows that female and male attributes are evident and equally exist in nature. So a greater wealth of meaning is found in the God whose love communicates life, maintains life, restores life, bestows fecundity, in short nourishes life completely.

Now to Bernard of Clairvaux—a man of moderate intellect, strong conviction, and immense force. He cared nothing for science or philosophy. He accepted the Bible

13

as God's word, for otherwise life would be a desert of dark uncertainty.[6] It is Bernard's controlled use of female imagery that guided the Church to desert any substantial theological development that the nature of God could conceivably include a female essence. For Bernard, such theological development would only find an arid place within the Church; and yet today, there are many within the Church who are pleading for that refreshing oasis where God our very Mother nourishes and refreshes us in Her caring. The Abbot of Clairvaux's usage of metaphorical language only allows God to possess feminine attributes. He has no difficulty allowing feminine metaphors to be applied to God to assist his expressions that elaborate certain attributes of the Godhead, but it is the masculine metaphor and the use of masculine language that legitimizes the real and desired picture of God.

In this Bernard reveals the limiting factor of his theology. He teases us with feminine metaphorical appeasements in his theological discussions, which fall short of declaring that God is our Mother. Bernard also has an extremely pessimistic view of creation. It is difficult to conclude from his work that personkind is created good. Personkind is created with all the carnal results of original sin; thus, he maintains, that personkind needs to submit to a transformation in which there shall be experienced a change from carnal things to things spiritual.[7] Before any good can happen, change must take place; and such change is recognized through a soteriological nurturing from the full breasts of the crucified. "For your breasts are better than wine, smelling sweet of best ointments."[8] Bernard associates nurturing with: Christ as the bridegroom for the joy to be attained from the nourishing breasts; with prelates as directors of souls receiving knowledge of how to rejoice with those who rejoice

14

and to be sad with those who sorrow (Romans 12:15); and finally Bernard views breasts and nursing as symbols of preaching and teaching.[9]

It is from that theological mind-set that Bernard steps into a specific discussion of God as Mother-nurturer. As his imagery is revealed, Bernard's nurturing imagery develops little further than that of an adolescent's fanatical fixation of the female form—especially breasts. Nurturing appears to be synonymous with suckling. The imagery of breasts and suckling may well be a mirror of what Bernard's society identified with nurturing. To suggest that a more complete understanding of nurturing includes protecting, caring, loving, and the act of providing sustenance as God-Mother acts seems to be a threatening concept in Cistercian theology. Certainly it could well be understood from that premise, that any image of God-Mother offering or giving creation those necessities of growth would be not only dangerous but absolute heresy. In his interpretation of the Song of Songs, we see that Bernard was playing it safe in presenting his maternal imagery. I am not suggesting that his theology would allow him to make any declaration of belief that God is our Mother, yet for Bernard nurturing vis-à-vis "breasts" are symbols used merely to describe a divine outpouring to others of affectivity or instruction.

The Song of Songs offers some vindication concerning how males in the authority of the Church should perform their tasks. The extent to which Bernard capitalizes on his mothering imagery is put forward in an administrative directive of pastoral care within the Cistercian order. But even here twelfth-century Cistercian theology would not accept a premise that the very essence of the "I AM WHO I AM" is the very nature of God our Mother. So many scholarly theologians like Bernard of

Clairvaux were so captivated by their own time and they were so protective of the male-controlled pastoral caring by the Church that these patriarchs would not flex their intellects to consider the great messages and teachings in the Old and New Testaments, and the Hebraic understandings of compassion. Had they seen such visions, they would have broken into "singing a new song in a strange land" that God is our Mother (Ps. 144:9).

At least the imagery of the womb of God and even Bernard's narrow concepts of nurturing could have led them into a greater magnitude of understanding of who God is. I suppose there remains that sense in which we should show no surprise at our frustration when the Church, in this last decade of the twentieth century, has shown a comparative slowness to encourage a growing theological awareness that God is our Mother. It is on this very point in theological thinking that Julian of Norwich issues the challenge to think again. As though announcing to the whole of personkind, she declares that there is so much more to be understood about God—from the Scriptures, from the early Christian writings—than what we have assumed to have been imposed upon us by a particular and current authoritarian interpretation.

Jacob wrestled with God; awakening from his dream, he marvelled at the experience. He never received an answer to his question, "Please tell me your name?" (Gen. 35:29). Jacob believed himself to have experienced the essence of a supernatural power. He was convinced that, by his own experience, he had been intimate with the true God; he had not just contacted the Infinite, but he had been involved with Yahweh. The place at which this wrestling took place, Jacob called Peniel. Through the course of history, no one has challenged that the name

16

of the place should be any other than "I have seen God face to face."

Moses stood before a burning bush and accepted without question that the I AM WHO I AM was speaking with him (Exod. 3:2). Traditionally that is the accepted name of God; it is accepted too that that Name was declared by Moses as the name by which God wished to be known. Jacob's question is now answered. Perhaps Moses attempted to make too much of this abstract nomenclature, but his relationship with God was so profound that he contemplated a God so sacred and powerful that it was sufficient to say "God is I Am"; God is a mystery; God knows man; God hates injustice, etc. Both Jacob and Moses experienced intimacy with God.

Julian, writing her revelation with such clarity and intensity, draws us into an experience that leaves the reader with no doubt that she was allowed to interpenetrate the very nature of God Herself. Her expression of the presence of the I AM WHO I AM is so inclusive that she discovered absolutely the living God-Mother. Julian's showings constitute one of the greatest reformations in the history of the theology of God.[10]

It would be a logical flow to this presentation to move directly into the revelations of "God is our very moder," which we received from Julian. But two important facts need to be emphasised: one, is that Julian affirms that she writes out of her own experiences; and second, that the reader is continuously cognisant of Julian's impeccable theology. First, Julian guarantees the authenticity and integrity of the whole sequence of revelations: ". . . and theyse thre be so onyd, as to my understondyng, that I can nott nor may deperte them. And by theyse thre as one I haue techyng whereby I ow to beleue and truste in oure lorde god, that of the same goodnesse that he shew it and for the same end, ryght so of the same goodnes and for the same end he shall declare it to us when it is his wyll."[11]

She takes great pains to show what is the substance and what are the modes of the showings as such, and which are her own insights and reflections.[12] The student of Julian is made to realize that if the content of Chapter 51 had not come to her as a revelation but merely through a meditation, it would not have been presented in its existing form. "For after 20 years [she writes] from the time of the revelation," she had difficulty with the allegory of the Lord and the Servant, and she describes how it was resolved by obedience and by faith that God showed it to her as "it is his wyll." There is a sense that we are "entering" a peculiar relationship with God in the showings, and with Julian herself as we pursue the evidence as recorded in her writings. Julian understands that she has been with God and she is utterly convinced of this—so much so that she is shameless as she shares that personal experience with us.

But somtyme it comyth to oure mynde that we haue prayde long tyme, and zett it thyngkyth vs that we haue nott oure askyng. But here fore shulde we nott be hevy, for I am suer by oure lordes menyng that eyther we a byde a better tyme, or more grace, or a better zyfte. Be wylle that we haue true knowyng in hym sekfe that he is beyng; and in thys knowyng he wylle that oure vnderstandyng be groundyd with alle oure myghtes and alle oure intent and alle our menyng. And by the gracious lyght of hym selfe he wylle that we haue vnderstandyng of thre thynges that folow. The furst is our noble and excelent makyng, the seconde oure precious and derwurthy agayne beyng, the thyrde althyng that he hath made beneth vs to serue vs and for oure loue kepyth it. Than menyth he thus, as if he seyde: Beholde and se that I haue done alle thys before thy prayer, and now thou arte and prayest me.[13]

Second, emphasis is on her impeccable development of theology. Whether or not she knows the scholastic term *communicato idiomutum* is for the most apt doctrinist to determine. The point is her belief in the substance of her message is irrefutable. One example of this is her theological progression concerning the suffering of God. She is insistent that God suffered and experienced pain mentally, physically, and spiritually. "The soore that he toke was oure flesch, in whych as sone he had felyng of dededly paynes."[14] Reading the paragraphs preceding this quote and the passages which follow, one feels that it is due to Julian's mind for such detail, and by her sensitivity in effectively conveying it that one has little option but to give serious respect to her authorship. This quick examination leads one to admit that Julian is quite capable of producing theological insights similar to those revealed in the Old Testatment treatise "Hosea." Her description of the concept that God suffered (and suffers) uses such immense emotion that it becomes easier for a theologian to accept with greater integrity the comment/ question: "Must God suffer if personkind is to be redeemed!?"

Julian tenaciously presents us with the revelation that "God is our very moder." There is so much excitement in her declaration that one is reminded of the eighth strope or vision in Deuteronomy-Isaiah (Isa. 65:17–19). This showing brings to the Lady of Norwich a time of great joy and peace; and it is in this joy and peace that she gains a clearer understanding of God's essence. In this revelation there comes, for her, a new

19

creation and a new age. The meaning here is not that the present world will be destroyed and a new world created, but rather that this present world will be changed. God can no longer be seen in the terms that His/Her creatures continue to give Her/Him, while at one and the same time ignoring the essence within the nature of God transmitted by the use of Her/His original and true name.

No longer is God to be bound by patriarchal, androcentric, and misogynistic concepts. The name first heard by Moses and subsequently proclaimed by him reveals the interrelatedness and equality that is to permeate creation and that unites Her with what She has made. I AM WHO I AM, in its simplicity, is a beautiful name for God. At the risk of blasphemy, it appears that even God could not name Herself more adequately for all to comprehend absolutely. It allows us to come into contact with and relate to the reality of God.

In the longer version of her showings, Julian's intelligence and sharpness of mind attests to the reality of God expressed through that Hebraic name. As Julian becomes so involved with the God-Mother imagery, she struggles to clearly tender her position that "god enjoyeth that he is our moder"; there is a sense that she becomes almost speechless in her descriptions. Words seem to pale in experiencing the vibrancy of being with God our Mother. As this anchoress works through a process to mould and to meld together the nature of God-Mother and to present this teaching to her audience in a comprehensible form, it is possible to become lost in her phraseology.

A metaphor that may help us understand something of what Julian experienced, is to compare this with the pictures that are seen in a kaleidoscope. Most children become enthralled with the imagery seen through this simple toy. For adults there is still a fascination that compels our minds to wonder at the mysterious patterns shaped by the pieces of glass. The kaleidoscope as a toy never changes; but to turn it, to see the individual glass pieces focused, to have presented a different pattern within itself, and to discover the new image fills the viewer with delight and serenity. Eventually the person may even come to realize that each piece is dependent upon the other. All pieces are a part of the entity of the kaleidoscope. Should but one piece be lost, broken, or retrieved from the kaleidoscope, then the nature of this instrument of delight and peace is no more. No longer can the viewer experience the wholeness of the toy even though a particular pattern has not been enjoyed.

So Julian has experienced God in a manner that previously no other person has in creation. She points out the additional greatness of God; she is turning creation to reveal what she has seen of the greater nature of our Mother. Julian, I am convinced, turned, as it were, and discovered another image of the nature of God. In Her substance, in Her nature, Julian sees God—She is our Father/Creator, She is our Lord/Redeemer, She is our Spirit/Comforter/Nurturer.

Many previous authors writing about Julian were content to see the Mother image of God as existing within the Trinity; and that Mother could not exist outside of the Trinity; nor could She be considered to exist as outside the Trinity or that She could not even be discussed as a vital part of the nature of the Godhead outside of the Trinity, i.e., She could not exist in any cognitive way on Her own merit. This is partially true; the Church developed the Trinitarian theology of the Godhead, maintaining that there exists an indissoluble bonding relationship between Father-Son-Holy Spirit. But, too, the

Church has in theology equally maintained that there is a value, an essence of Father-ness, Son-ness, Holy Spiritness each within the very nature of God to been seen and experienced alone.

Although some may consider such statements as dangerous theology, to state that one cannot discuss or experience Father/Son/Holy Spirit separately is ludicrous. For that is the very stuff of which theology is made; to give human expression to the Godhead, to experience an individual relationship with the Godhead as Creator, Redeemer, Comforter. This author maintains that Julian has nudged the kaleidoscope a little further and has given the Church another view of the I AM WHO I AM; here is God our Mother. Julian is bolder than that; she states that God our Mother is the bonding person of the Godhead that gives expression and enhances the very Trinity.

Austin Cooper arrives at the same conclusion, yet one may consider that he is patronizing Julian. He does not. I believe that in his comments on Chapter 60 of Julian's longer version, he wants us to recognize that the anchoress is revealing to us the God as our Mother. "The word of God is basically a homely and courteous thing. Julian is so right to see it so aptly summed up in this fine and lovely word, 'mother.' "[15] This is a lovely word; the meaning of the word itself has such value that it is seemingly endless. But its meaning can hold a violent reality for some. It does send the patriarchal, misogynist part of society screaming to its knees as the full understanding of She our Father/Creator is revealed. "The Looking Glass War" of Mary Daly and the interdependence of Mother in Julian may at first be seen as in opposition; nonetheless they are complements of the same existence.[16]

Mary Daly is violent in making a case for the feminine in God; Julian's exploitation of God our Mother presents the reality of personkind's experience, even though man has ignored much of the experience. Julian joins a biblical tradition concerning the nature of God, and this becomes an integral part of her shorter and longer versions; but what is more significant, she leaves us a valued legacy. God through her has unveiled a particular richness of Her nature and Julian challenges us to find the I AM WHO I AM. God is Mother. The hypothesis begs us to question in what sense is God not merely parental but actually Mother.

Mother has a most important bonding nature, which makes mother the closest of kin to children. Mother gives freely love to the child in a mysterious way, which is mostly misunderstood by the rest of creation and consequentially viciously maligned. Mother has the capability of putting into place, most appropriately, the relatedness between good and evil and thereby enables guidance to be given to life in such a fashion that the purpose of life becomes attainable. This is motherhood for Julian. This is what she experienced through her revelations. What other expression, what other reality is to be declared than "and thus I saw that god enjoyeth that he is our moder. . . ."

Julian continues in her revelations with an astounding announcement, i.e., we are to be brought to Fatherhood through the Motherhood of Jesus.[17] This is one of the lady's most complex statements. It is Jesus' Motherhood that brings us to the Father's joy to which the risen Jesus was restored, and thus recalls the promise that "alle shall be welle, and alle shall be welle, and all manner of thyng shall be welle." Her theology here may seem astounding and complex, but she is being extremely precise. Motherhood—"God is oure very moder"—is so absolute to the essence of the I AM that She (God our Mother) has the status of real and penultimate existence. In this anchoress's teachings, Motherhood is rooted in the I AM WHO I AM and is coterminous with the Father and the Spirit.

> For the furst I saw and vnderstode that pe hygh myght of the trynyte is oure fader, and the depe wysdom of the trynyte is oure moder, and the grete loue of the trynyte is oure lorde; and alle these haue we in kynde and in oure substanncyall makyng. And ferthere more I saw that the seconde person, whych is oure moder, substanncyally the same derewurthy person, is now become oure moder sensuall, for we be doubell of gods makyng, that is to sey substanncyall and sensuall. Oure substyannce is pe hyer perty, whych we haue in oure fader god almyghty; and the seconde person of the trynyte is oure moder in kynd in oure substanncyall makyng, in whom we be groundyd and rotyd, and he is oure moder of mercy in our sensualyte takyng. And thus oure moder is to vs dyverse manner werkyng, in whom oure pertys be kepte vndepertyd; for in oure moder Cryste we profyt and encrese, and in mercy he reformyth vs and restoryth, and by the vertu of his passion, his deth and his vprsyng onyd vs to oure substannce.[18]

There are those who have difficulties placing Jesus as central to the Motherhood of God as Julian has demonstrated. If feminine images of God cannot be rejected, then it may become easier for those critics, in a framework of antifeminism, to connect that image with the Holy Spirit, who is hidden, who did not appear historically, and who manifests love.[19]

Such a statement is unworthy of the Julian showings; Julian is interested in merely declaring a female attachment to the Godhead. She is proclaiming a vibrant, honest, and incisive revelation of another part of the full essence of God. For Julian, there is the full recognition that God is our Mother and of Her equality and position within the Godhead, even though there are references in her longer version in which she appropriates Her to the second Person of the Trinity. There is no need to give a gender to God. There is no need for us to say there is only a Trinity. There is no need to captivate God in an entity of some people's insistence of how She/He is to be seen or contemplated. There is no need to cage, tame, or train God to our own liking into Something "that is really far too big ever to be forced into little man-made boxes with neat labels upon them."[20]

To do so is to put God in a box. The discoveries of Jacob, Moses, Julian, of physical and biological science, astronomy and psychology, the rising of feminine equality and status have persevered to profoundly influence people's conception of the nature and "size" of God. Thank Her for that!! As J. B. Phillips stated some forty years ago, if there be a wisdom behind the immense complexities of the phenomena that all can observe, then it is that of a God tremendous in (Her) power and wisdom. It is emphatically not a little God.[21]

It is certainly not a gender to be awarded the Creator, the Redeemer, the Nurturer about which Julian is speaking when she writes:

Verely as god is oure fader, as verely is god oure moder; and that shewde he in all, and namely in theyse swete wordys there he seyth: I it am; that is to sey: I it am, the myght and the goodnes of faderhode, I it am, the wysdom

and the kyndes of moderhode, I it am, the lyght and the
grace that is all blessyd loue; I it am, the trynyte, I it am,
pe vnyte; I it am, the hye souereyn goodnesse of all manner thyng, I it am that makyth the to (loue, I it am pat
makith pe to) long, I it am, the endless fullfyng of all true
desyers.[22]

It is quite acceptable and quite thinkable that Our
Mother has a purpose that is being worked out in concert
with Her creation on the stage of this small planet, which
She is continuously nurturing and redeeming. It is even
plausible to believe that She was the prime mover to
reduce Herself to the stature of created humanity in order
to visit earth as the Word became flesh. All Christians
affirm that historical reality. The sort of thing that is
outrageous and that borders insanity is to dismiss
through arguments premised on patriarchal and misogynist interpretations is Julian's truth that God is our
Mother. I accept and believe the gift given to us in her
revelations. Personkind is overdue to take the God-box
off the shelf of misinterpretations, open the lid, and let
God out to be rediscovered. She is Father, He is Mother.
She/He is Nurturer and the Sophia-Wisdom.

Notes

1. Edmund Colledge and James Walsh, ed., *A Book of Showings
to the Anchoress Julian of Norwich,* vol. 2 (Toronto: Pontifical Institute of Medieval Studies, 1978) 502. "Mercy is a pyttefull properte,
whych longyth to moderhode in tender loue." (Mercy is a compassion
which belongs to the tender love of motherhood.)
2. Ibid., page 592. Translation: "And so is Jesu our very mother
in our nature, from our creation [making for she made us], and he is
our true mother in grace because [she] took our created nature [upon
herself] . . . I understand three ways of seeing motherhood in God:

26

first is ground of our created nature, the second is assumption of our nature [taking our nature], and the beginning of the motherhood of grace, the third is I was aware of motherhood working [in him]." The brackets are mine.

3. Numbers 11:12; Psalms 17:8; 48:7; Isaiah 12:3; 62:5; 66:13; Matthew 33:37; Luke 15:8–9 . . . to mention only a few references in Scripture.

4. The sixty-sixth chapter of this prophet's writings is an excellent example among many. The Israel nation is returning from exile; the task of rebuilding Jerusalem is to begin. The renewal of faith in (Yahweh) God is equally a part of the nation's rejuvenation. Therefore, "I will extend prosperity to her like a river, and the wealth of the nations like an overflowing stream; and you shall nurse and be carried on her arm, and dandled on her knees. As a mother comforts her child, so I will comfort you; you shall be comforted in Jerusalem. You shall see, and your heart shall rejoice; your bodies shall flourish like the grass."

5. It is argued by some whether Jesus ever did attend rabbinical school. This statement can be challenged with some legitimacy. On this point my belief follows the traditional thought that argues that Jesus did in fact attend rabbinical school.

6. Will Durant, *The Story of Civilization: The Age of Faith,* vol. iv (New York: Simon & Schuster, 1950) 790.

7. Bernard of Clairvaux, *On the Song of Songs II,* vol. iii, trans. Kilian Walsh (Kalamazoo, Michigan: Cistercian Publications, 1983) Sermon 39.

Etienne Gilson, *The Mystical Theology of St. Bernard,* trans. by W. H. C. Downes (Kalamazoo, Michigan: Cistercian Publications, 1990) 73–84.

8. Ibid., Sermons 1 and 9.

9. Caroline Walker Bynum, *Jesus as Mother* (Berkeley, Los Angeles, London: University of California Press, 1982) 117–8, and op. cit., Sermons 23, 41.

10. Caroline Walker Bynum, *Jesus as Mother* (Berkeley, Los Angeles, London: University of California Press, 1982) chapter 4.

11. Edmund Colledge and James Walsh, editors, *A Book of Showings to the Anchoress Julian of Norwich,* vol. 2 (Toronto: Pontifical Institute of Mediaeval Studies, 1978), chapter 51, page 520. Translation: "and by these three and one as to my understanding, that I cannot nor may separate them and by these three and one I have been taught to owe belief and trust that our Lord God, through that same goodness that he showed it and for the same end [reason], he shall declare it to us when it is his will [when he desires it to be revealed]." The brackets are mine.

12. Ibid., 520.

13. Ibid., chapter 42, pages 469–71. Translation: "But sometime it comes to our mind that we have prayed a long time, and still that we have not any answer. But here we should not be [sorry] at this for I am sure our Lord means that either we are to pray at a better [more suitable] time, or more grace, or a better gift. He wills that we have true knowledge of himself that he is the all-being; and in this knowledge he wills that our understanding be grounded [with] all our might and all our intent and all our sincerity. And by the gracious light of himself he wills that we have understanding of the three following things. The first is noble and excellence of our creation, the second is the preciousness and value of our redemption, the third everything [in creation] is to serve us and out of love for us [he made/keeps it]. This is his meaning, as if he said: look and see that I have done all this before your prayers and now you are [exist] and [are] to pray to me." The brackets are mine.

14. Ibid., chapter 51, page 540, lines 280–82. This translation is mine: "The pain that he took was our flesh, in which as [God] he had feeling of deadly [mortal] pain."

15. Austin Cooper, *Julian of Norwich* (Mystic, Conn.: Twenty-third Publications, 1988) 104.

16. Mary Daly, *Beyond God the Father* (Boston: Beacon Press, 1985) 193–98.

17. Edmund Colledge and James Walsh, ed., *A Book of Showings to the Anchoress Julian of Norwich*, vol. 2 (Toronto: Pontifical Institute of Mediaeval Studies, 1978) 613.

18. Ibid., pages 585–86. Translation: "For the first I saw and understood the great might [power] of the Trinity is our Father, and the deep wisdom of the Trinity is our Mother, and the great love of the Trinity is our Lord. And all these we have in kind and in our substantial [essential] making [creation]. Furthermore I saw that the second person which is our Mother, substantially [essential] the beloved person is now become our Mother sensual [in our sensual nature]. For we be twice of God's making that is to say substantially [essential] and sensual [in our sensual nature] our substance [being] is the high part which we have in our Father God almighty; and the second person of the Trinity is our Mother in kind in our substantially [essential] making in whom we are grounded and rooted and he is our Mother in mercy in our sensual [nature] talking [on herself/himself] and thus our Mother describes to us diverse manners [in which she] works in whom by your prayers we be kept undeparted [. . . in whom we are together even if the ways separate us]; for in our Mother Christ we grow and increase and in mercy he [she] reforms us and restores and by the virtue of his passion, death, and his resurrection he is one with us in our substance [being]." The brackets are mine.

19. Ritamary Bradley, *Julian's Way* (London: Harper Collins Religious, 1992) 144.

20. J. B. Phillips, *Your God is Too Small* (London: The Epworth Press, 1958) 36.

21. Ibid., 37. The parentheses are mine.

22. Edmund Colledge and James Walsh, ed., *A Book of Showings to the Anchoress Julian of Norwich,* vol. 2 (Toronto: Pontifical Institute of Mediaeval Studies, 1978), 590. Translation: "As truly as God is our Father; as truly is God our Mother; and that he showed all this and namely in these sweet words when he said: I am it. That is to say, I am, the might [power] and goodness of Fatherhood; I am, the wisdom and kindness of Motherhood; I am, the light and the grace that is all blessed love; I am, the Trinity; I am, unity; I am the high sovereign goodness of all manner of things; I am, that makes [enables you] to love; I am, makes you [enables you] to long [yearn]; I am, the endless fulfilling [eternal satisfaction] of all true desires." The brackets are mine.

3

"Sophia-Wisdom": The Second Challenge

To discover anew Sophia-Wisdom is the task of this hypothesis. "Truth seeth god, and wysdom beholdyth god, and of theyse two comyth the thurde, and that is a mervelous delyght in god, whych is loue. Where truth and wysdom is, verely there is loue, verely comyng of the both, and alle of goddes makyng. For god is endlesse souereyne truth, endlesse souereyne wysdom, endlesse souereyne loue vnmade."[1] This quote from the forty-fourth chapter of Revelation 14 in Julian's longer version recalls the sayings of Solomon recorded in Proverbs 8:22–31. The significance of this passage is its portrayal of Wisdom's part in Creation.[2]

Wisdom is of eternity, and Wisdom is forming all things in creation. Proverbs is not considered a part of the Wisdom literature in Hebraic Scriptures, but here we are informed of the status that the Hebrew nation acknowledges Wisdom; She is part of divinity. She is not attributed necessarily to any person of the Trinity, but is divinity (I AM WHO I AM) characterized and revealed in the creativity of God. In Hebraic theology, just as each of the Trinity (Father, Son, and Spirit) is not God alone, so Wisdom is to be experienced not as an entity in Her own right, even though poetical descriptions in the Old

Testament writings tend to depict Her as having an independent existence.

Reading Ecclesiasticus 24: 1–7), it is shown that Wisdom is personified as coming out of the Godhead and being among all nations: "I sought a resting place in whose territory should I abide." It is in Israel where She reaches concrete expression and recognition within the divine. She has a firm root, She is trustworthy, She is with the I AM WHO I AM. This identification is clear and definite. The revelation of Sinai is the supreme manifestation of Wisdom, argues Wheeler Robinson, for She is the concrete expression of the beginning, the fullness, the crown, and the root of God.[3]

Consequently, it is logical to see Hebrew thought accepting that there is a hypostasis here and clearly a characteristic transformation of Wisdom into a most cherished manifestation of God. Again we see Wisdom as an immanent divine presence shown in the Book of the Wisdom of Solomon (7:22–8:1):

> For wisdom, the fashioner of all things, taught me. There is in her a spirit that is intelligent, holy, unique, manifold, subtle, mobile, clear, unpolluted, distinct, invulnerable, loving the good, keen, irresistible, beneficent, humane, steadfast, sure, free from anxiety, all-powerful through all spirits that are intelligent, pure, and altogether subtle. For wisdom is more mobile than any motion; because of her pureness she pervades and penetrates all things. For she is a breath of the power of God, and a pure emanation of the glory of the Almighty; therefore nothing defiled gains entrance into her. For she is a reflection of eternal light, a spotless mirror of the working of God, and an image of his goodness. Although she is but one, she can do all things, and while remaining in herself, she renews all things; in every generation she passes into holy souls

31

and makes them friends of God, and prophets; for God loves nothing so much as the person who lives with wisdom. She is more beautiful than the sun, and excels every constellation of the stars. Compared with the light she is found to be superior, for it is succeeded by the night, but against wisdom evil does not prevail. She reaches mightily from one end of the earth to the other, and she orders all things well.

This is a remarkable, striking passage, revealing a sense that the author radiates a most profound spiritual insight into the very essence of God; to have this recorded within the canon of Scripture and within a patriarchal-dominated society of Judaism in the 145th year B.C. is even more astounding. On the other hand, such revelation gives an added emphasis to proclamations and records that the I AM WHO I AM is very much at work with all people as well as being a part of their experience of God. She who is our Mother issued this same revelation described by Julian's "showings." As we shall see, perhaps Julian visioned even more of God's essence, as her showings unfolded more of the prophetic revelations in the Wisdom of Solomon. Here the nature of Wisdom is spirit, holy, unique, pure, kind, loving, omniscient, omnipresent, and even pervades the spirits/souls of personkind. This apocryphal document (chapters 4–7) states further the concept of Wisdom: She can do all things, and abiding within herself, She renews all things and enters into the lives of people, makes them friends of God and is the vehicle of inspiration.

Before leaving this fascinating piece of revelation of Julian in "truth seeth god, and wisdom beholdyth god . . .," there is more to consider as this attempts to clarify the text in Proverbs. The text from Proverbs reads: "The Lord created me in the beginning of his way . . . ," but should it not read, "The Lord possessed me at the beginning of his work. . . ." It is possible that here we have a paradigm of patriarchal translation. Paradigm is a form or model; when a translation is made to fit a model, then the danger exists that intellectual and spiritual growth is stunted or prohibited. If one wishes to maintain control, power, and authority, then only those elements that can possibly fit the model would be admitted to the model.

The Hebrew word *qanah* can be translated "possessed" or "created"; it is one of those Hebraic expressions that has a duality of interpretation. Such translation then should not prohibit other expressions when those expressions contradict androcentric thought. For this author, ". . . the Lord possessed wisdom in the beginning of his way . . ." is a more accurate concept, and a more appropriate translation, as we discover the richness of Julian as she awakens us to a fuller understanding of the I AM WHO I AM. Wisdom was present at, and Wisdom is present in creation as an integral part of the mystery of God's nature; She becomes equal with God in creation. Therefore, as with God, so it is with Wisdom; She was before all.

As part of this hypothesis is to discover anew the treasures of Wisdom, the early Christian writings should be the object for some investigation. For this exercise the choice is to review noncanonical (New Testament) writing. Obviously part of the Wisdom literature holds strong convictions about Wisdom. Although the manuscripts can be difficult to read, the Gospel of Thomas recalls the unique regard the Church exhibited for Wisdom by directing its members on many occasions to the Book of Ecclesiasticus. Thomas insists that there may be several stages involved in seeking and finding Wisdom; but once found, Thomas makes it emphatically clear that it is She who leads people to the Kingdom. Recalling the story of "the sower who went out to sow seed" (Matthew 13: 3–9 and Mark 4:2–9, and Luke 8:4–8), Thomas writes a slightly different version; and again there is a link to Wisdom: "Come to Wisdom as one who plows and sows and wait for her good crops. For in her work you will toil a little and soon you will eat of her produce."

This Wisdom directs and gives vitality to her creation. But more than this, there is a collage of thoughts that comes together through the influence of Thomas. This gathering of thought is from several people who have discovered the Sophia-Wisdom: Solomon, Thomas, John, an unknown Manichean poet, and Julian of Norwich:

Wisdom is more noble than any motion.
    I bore them up and they
    wore me as a garment
    upon them.

because of her pureness she (Wisdom)
pervades and penetrates all things.
    I am in all, I bear the heavens
    I am the foundation, I support
    the earths.

For she is breath of the power of God,
and a pure emanation of the glory
of the Almighty;

Therefore nothing defiled gains
entrance into her (Wisdom).
For she is a reflection of eternal
working of God and an image
of his goodness.

> I am the light that shines
> forth,
> I am the light of the world
> whoever follows he will never
> walk in darkness but will have
> light of life.
> I am (Wisdom is), the light
> that makes the souls rejoice.

Although she is but one, she (wisdom)
can do all things, and while remaining
in herself she renews all things;

> I am the life of the world,
> I am the milk that is in all
> trees,
> I am the sweet water that is
> under the children of matter.

In every generation she passes into
holy souls and makes them friends of
God, and prophets;

for God loves nothing as much as the
person who lives with her (wisdom).

She (wisdom) reaches mightily from one
end of the earth to the other;

And she (wisdom) orders all things
well.

To end this collage, we hear Julian's proclamation:

All shall be well, and all shall
be well, and all manner of thing
shall be well.

Julian through her showings calls us to review the Sophia-Wisdom-God. Studying the writing of this anchoress, the student comes crashing down from antiquated theological pedestals into the reality of wrestling within his or her own experience concerning the essence of the nature of God. It is not to develop a Sophia-Wisdom-God theological treatise that Julian is exacting here, but from a pure, simple, mustard-seed scenario to discern who She (Wisdom) is. Although the idea is pure and simple, the consequence and conclusion are profound. We realize that Julian entwines Sophia-Wisdom throughout the record of her revelation and in fact manipulates her readers to resolve the question, "Who is Sophia-Wisdom?"

Being exposed more and more to Julian's "showings," one finds that she sharpens the student's awareness of the presence of Sophia-Wisdom within the essence of God. By her explicit revelations Julian records, and through reinforcement of plentiful references to Scripture—suddenly—one is captivated by the very presence of Wisdom. She is the interwoveness of the fabric or nature of God. She is no partial aspect of God, but consciously, and with some ease, it is clear that Sophia is an integral part of the wholeness in an indeterminable way; such is this interdependence that she is seen as the very personification of God as God experienced in the expectations and drudgeries and in the happiness and sorrows of personkind. Realizing this confirms the need to be more cognitive or intuitive concerning the language and inferences we relate when speaking of Sophia.

In our society even the pronoun "she" is used to denote existence, rights, and the place given to personkind.

Such language can be patronizing toward the subject about which we are speaking. Even to use theological language, which remains framed in androcentric idealism, "she" can be dangerous; we must take care not to cause another to translate language in such a way as to give even the slightest indication that we are inferring a patriarchal substitution. That would be demeaning and, in turn, would engage a degradation of the essence of the I AM WHO I AM, which could be construed as the final form of blasphemy.

However, to realize this interwoveness is not to identify Sophia with creation only, with Jesus only, or with the Spirit only, but is to uncover Sophia as a distinctive part of the Essence, of the I AM WHO I AM; and that Sophia's very quintessence is incorporated implicitly in everything we know of creation, redemption, and nurturing. She vivifies, knits together, and upholds life in pervading and unquenchable love.[4]

Some attempt to legitimize Sophia-Wisdom's place in the Godhead by employing the phrase "the One Who Is." The difficulty with this substitutive phrase is just that—it is a substitution. This is a type of patronizing that tends to nullify the attribute that God is personal. To introduce such a name or title causes the eventual intellectual absenting of the personae in the Godhead and causes a disregard toward all the natural attributes experienced through the imagery of Creator, Redeemer, and Nurturer. Substitution phraseology such as this tends to increase the risk of an extreme negativity directed toward the imagery of the deity. Then what would become of developing further the value and ethical appreciation of our history? Of obtaining comprehensive knowledge concerning relationships between nations and/or between beautiful peoples and civilizations? Of expanding an understanding of ourselves through the continual evaluation of the greatness seen in the ancient peoples and in the Hebrew People? And of determining in the most ethical and moral way the status, position, and valued propensity of all persons?

Julian's forcefulness is intended to have us become more aware of who She/He is through the disciplined phraseology and imagery. This adds significance to the prophecy; to know God is to know personkind and to know the depths of personkind is to know more about the nature of God. Julian's revelation of Mother and equally of Sophia-Wisdom allows us to uncover Her/Him by opening the box into which She has been placed for centuries.

There is another fundamental truth about Sophia-Wisdom and that concerns the value we give to community. "She who is: linguistically is possible; theologically is legitimate; existentially and religiously is necessary if speech about God [Sophia-Wisdom] is to shake off the shackles of idolatry and be a blessing for women. In the present sexist situation, where structures and language, praxis and personae attitudes convey an ontology of inferiority to women, naming toward God [Sophia-Wisdom] in this way is a gleam of light on the road to genuine community."[5]

Rather, this author would prefer to say that naming of God in this way is as a bolt of light directing us into a more sincere expression of community, and that through the conceptualization of such naming, all personkind will come to realize that the value and efficacy of community is found in the genuine performance of equality between the sexes.

Julian's multidescriptions of Sophia-Wisdom is the motivation through which we perceive Sophia as the interwovenness of the Godhead's nature. These are fairly

powerful verbal sketches that can cause some confusion.[6]
Her writing about this relationship can leave the impression that ghostlike Sophia meanders in and out of the Godhead. One can almost envision an "airy-fairy-mist-like-scarlet-pimpernel-mentality" invading Julian's otherwise precise, but practical, theological concepts. Sophia-Wisdom is depicted as everyone and no one. She is a moving, brooding entity, permeating everything touched but is seen vanishing away, leaving everything to resolve personal perceptions and activities.

This lady of Norwich, this author believes, has left to us an image of the Godhead as much more than that kind of mysterious hovering entity leaving our lives, at times, only moisturized by a spiritual or intellectual wetting. Julian reiterates that God is God; Julian confirms most emphatically that which many have forgotten—that God (Sophia-Wisdom) broods over and permeates creation, redemption, and nurturing all. We have heard this and read this many times in many places in the history of the Ancients as recorded in the Old Testament. But we have suppressed or ignored these delineations. She enters everything and everywhere (Ps. 139:7–8) weeps over the misuse and wasting of creation or the environment and as an integral part of the creation process enables a newness to commence.

Through her "showings," Julian's treatment of the sacrifice of Jesus and by her telling of the servant parable, she sees Wisdom pouring energy from Herself into life.[7] Julian allows the student's imagination to picture this as Sophia-Wisdom entering an arena to wrestle the forces of violence and meaninglessness. Sophia-Wisdom, the victorious one, enables renewal to take place, bringing peace and restoring life into unimaginable and equitable values. The meaning of *peace* carries the same sense

39

as the old Hebraic *shalom*. This comprehensive word denotes "total well-being," "harmony," "the harmonious community" in which full growth of personkind can be attained.

This author is convinced that Sophia-Wisdom, for Julian, could be experienced as the interwovenness of the nature of personkind just as She is within the Godhead. Personkind accepting the status of interdependence in or the interwoveness of Sophia-Wisdom and living within existing relationships has the ability and capability to develop and grow into completeness. It is upon that exhibition of harmony, agreement, and psychic community that the foundation of life exists. That is the optimum desire of Sophia-Wisdom for Her creation. So it is in every generation that She possesses that ability to make people friends of God, just as Moses was a personal friend of God. To weave God and personkind into a relationship that grows from one understanding into another, Julian gives this image of Sophia-Wisdom using numerous pictures from the Old Testament.[8]

In her "showings," the anchoress reminds us again and again that it is "God oure very moder" with the aegis of "Wysdom" who has the authority and power of making personkind co-workers in the Godhead's redeeming purpose, i.e., each are co-workers (with God) promoting each other to maintain community.

Finally, Julian challenges the place we have opted to give to the historical Jesus. She seems to be saying that we have appeased patriarchal interpretations and standards. No apology need be declared that the God-Mother-Spirit-Sophia-Wisdom became personified in the form of a man called Jesus. Granted that was in all probability the most convenient and easiest form by which She could enter creation and at one and the same time receive serious attention from the population. Perhaps God could not work through creation using any other model at that specific point in creation, but that is no reason to ignore or suppress the fulness or the essence of the Godhead by paying service to patriarchal and androcentric individualism.

The immoveability of androcentric thought had so impregnated the mentality of humankind that only a man-Jesus would be tolerated. It is worth repeating a most provoking understatement that had God become a person in the form of a woman, "She would certainly have been greeted with a colossal shrug." For this latter part of the twentieth century, Julian has forced a reopening of the Scriptures in every era and in every progression of Hebraic development. To discover Sophia-Wisdom through Julian's "Showings" is to experience new exhilaration toward Christanity beyond what one can imagine; for example, the merchant who reportedly found a pearl of great value and went and sold all that he had and bought it exhibits that extraordinary excitement.

Obviously this stimulus is shared by others: "if someone would argue that humankind could be saved only by the incarnation of the Word in maleness, although I could not accept the argument, I would still find some meaning in it, since throughout history men have far outstripped women in domineering attitudes. Hence, it might be appropriate, according to our own limited human thinking, that Christ became a man to break the fetters of sexism by His absolute humility and liberty for others. Surely, anyone who wants to overemphasize Christ's maleness in order to establish prerogatives of males over females has not understood Jesus as the liberator of all people, men and women, and has not understood the way he liberated us."[9]

We miss the illumination of the Gospel if we fail to realize that the core difficulty is not with the man-Jesus but that more men do not exemplify the image into whom they are made. It is a pity that patriarchy seemingly wins out; for it is patriarchy that defines their self-identity and relationship rather identifying with all that is Sophia-Wisdom interwoven in God's essence. To reread any part of Scripture with any scrap of common sense uncovered in "feminist hermeneutics makes it possible to affirm that despite subsequent distortion something more than the subordination of women is possible, for Jesus-Sophia's story of ministry, suffering, final victory, and new community signify love, grace, and shalom for everyone equally, and for the outcast, including women most of all."[10]

Notes

1. Ibid., pages 483–84. Translation: "Truth sees God; and wisdom [looks at] beholds God; and from these two comes the third, and that is a marvellous delight in God, which is love. Where there is truth and wisdom truly there is love, truly coming from them both; and all of goodness' making. For God is endless [eternal] sovereign truth, endless [eternal] sovereign wisdom, endless [eternal] sovereign love, unmade [not created]."

2. For a complete explanation of this author's concept of "Wisdom" and for scriptural references and documentation, see Appendix I; W. O. E. Oesterley and Theodore H. Robinson, *An Introduction to the Books of the Old Testament* (London: S. P. C. K., 1955); Theodore H. Robinson, *A History of Israel,* vol. i. (Oxford: Clarendon Press, 1955); W. O. E. Oesterley, *A History of Israel,* vol. ii. (Oxford: Clarendon Press, 1955).

3. H. Wheeler Robinson, *Inspiration and Revelation in the Old Testament* (Oxford: Clarendon Press, 1956) 260. The meaning of *root* here is "firm" or "trustworthy." Thus, she is the concrete expression of . . . the crown and the root (the firmness and/or trustworthiness) of God. Wisdom is and continues to be and will remain the effluence (the

pouring out) and effulgence (the splendor of the diffusing of the flood of light) of God.

4. Elizabeth A. Johnson, *She Who Is* (New York: Crossroad Publishing Co., 1992) 135.

5. Ibid., 243.

6. Edmund Colledge and James Walsh, ed., *Book of Showings to the Anchoress Julian of Norwich,* vol. 2 (Toronto: Pontifical Institute of Mediaeval Studies, 1978) chapter 53, lines 1–8, page 554. Here Julian uses Wisdom 10: 1–12 as a base reference or base text, recalling her experience, compares her own experience in relation to past theological reflection. Julian is so confident, she states that "we know" that "She [Sophia-Wisdom] preserves him . . . brought him out of sin . . . gives him power to govern all things." The "him" here refers to "personkind." The brackets are mine.

7. Several references have been made to "The Lord and the Servant" parable. For those who may find a reading helpful, a translation is recorded in Appendix II. If the reader is interested in another translation, *Julian of Norwich: Revelations of Divine Love* by Clifton Wolters is published through Penguin Press, 1966.

8. Exodus 33: 11; Psalms 123:2; Malachi 1:5–6.

9. Bernard Haring, *Free and Faithful in Christ* (New York: Crossroad Publications, 1984) 139.

10. Elizabeth A. Johnson, *She Who Is* (New York: Crossroad Publishing, 1992) 161.

4

To Learn Some Lessons from Julian: The Third Challenge

Spiders spinning silvery, silky sanctuaries are fascinating exhibitions of activity; so found Robert Bruce. This Scottish king, taking his own sanctuary in a cavern on the island of Rathlin, was inspired into renewed efforts by a spinning arachnid. The story is a well-known and famous piece of folklore. To classify this tale as historical presents not a few difficulties; yet, its telling, even in historical documents, has persisted for centuries. Scots answer the challenge that "the story cannot be proven" with the retort "it cannot be disproven." They are correct.

Robert was alone in self-imposed exile on Rathlin. Recounting his defeat in a recent skirmish on the Scottish mainland, he was trying to salvage from the near intimacy of a hopeless condition, new plans for another attempt to reestablish his kingdom. During this contemplation, his attention was interrupted by a spider struggling to weave a web above where he sat. This "wee thing" would stretch a long thread across a relatively large space only to have it snap asunder. But it would try again.

The man-wanting-to-be-king not only empathized with the spider's seeming hopeless situation, but felt great pity towards the creature. He compared their respective struggles. He was trying to stretch his rule across a desired kingdom only to have his efforts dashed by opposing forces. But here in the cave, he noticed that the spider worked on; the arachnid refused to give up. According to folklore, six times it tried, and on the seventh attempt, it succeeded. "Had he," wondered Robert, "tried six times, and failed six times?!" Should he give up, or make the seventh attempt? Would he become as good as the little spider and persevere and finally win a kingdom? Giving a grateful glance toward the wee spider, he left the cave, summoned his militia, and moved out to conquer his kingdom.

The importance of this story is its lesson of perseverance. But there is another lesson to be gained from Robert Bruce's eight-legged creature. The silvery spun network is worth a particular look. The spider has to complete its home, so it can live; so it can be nourished; so it can take part in creation by assisting in the continuance of its species. Any broken thread threatens its very existence, and every part of its social interaction will not be experienced. Thus, it tried numerous times to preserve its interdependence through a special interwovenness. Any broken strand destroys the essence of the webbed membrane. Consequently, the interdependent existence of the web to encourage and maintain the functions of its very life becomes jeopardized or, in the extreme, annihilated. Every allegory disintegrates with overextended applications and by making pictures too elaborate. Further use of this allegory resides with the reader with his/her development and new discovery.

There is an application extending out of this folklore for us. First, it is to emphasize that it is an awkward and arduous encounter to understand and finally accept

Julian's teaching of God our very Mother and of Sophia-Wisdom as the interwovenness of the Godhead. Second, it is anticipated that the transfer of learning into daily life will need "God-like" perseverance and "Job-like" patience. Tenacity will be necessary more than six times; rather it is expected to image the infinite Hebraic formula of "seventy times seven." Yet, there is that unrelenting push of mind and spirit that drives us to direct society into the acceptance of an infusion of the Nurturer, of mutual responsibility, of the eventual attainment of equality for all personkind and of interdependency, all with the Godhead through the teaching of Julian.

This third challenge from Julian's "showings" sees Sophia-Wisdom offering us the opportunity to grasp the understanding, the value, the exigency of creation, redemption, and nurturing and comforting. As previously stated, this challenge dares us to discover further that interdependence and equality are not new concepts or images—they are imbedded deeply in the teaching of Scripture about the nature of God our Mother, Sophia and personkind. Women and men in every nation and in every part of the Church, if they are not doing so, must search in unprecedented ways to discover how to serve as Christians and to fulfill the mission of our spiritual heritage in our world and in our personal lives. We need to radically study the form of our own obedience to mission and the needs it has to share in the one simple life and witness everywhere.

Mission here is interdependence, i.e., the mutual equal sharing, the mutually equal receiving. Society has given way too many times to spoken inferences and inflexible ideas about "older," "younger," "female," "male," "he," "she," "yours," "mine," and thereby given birth to what has become, consciously and unconsciously, determined as unreal and untrue, the efficacy that there exists an interdependency in and among personkind. Society has harboured and willfilly continues to entertain patriarchal and androcentric structures.

One lesson learned from previous hypotheses affects how we read the Scriptures, and how we identify additional or new messages while reading the Gospels. While reading Scripture often we succumb to androcentric intellectual programming that causes a mental warm fuzziness, prohibiting us to come to terms with the reality presented in the story or description of events. Many have become so conditioned by past male-made norms and male-dominated philosophy that other critical paths of instruction have become obliterated. Gatherings of male-only Church councils of the past assumed the role of Jesus' stand-in and through commentaries chose only explanations that appealed to their need for power. Some even in this century, forget that the Church, supposedly, is the extension of Jesus' life in the world, and if it is to be effective, all members of the Church must be models of the way Jesus lived.

Nobody was afraid of Jesus. Women and men followed him everywhere since they were made aware that Jesus understood their joy, their anguish, their pain. Sinners—personkind—felt comfortable with Jesus; their lives changed in time. Persons do not feel comfortable with the Church. Why? The model it has chosen is patriarchal, androcentric with legalistic and judgemental Jesus moulded in its own image. That frightens the sheep and drives them away and makes them afraid of the Godhead who creates, redeems, and nurtures.

Julian's revelation calls the Church back to what it is intended to become. The Church, i.e., the body of God on earth, is to be the medium of Jesus' message, not allowing that message and Jesus to get lost in its own politic. It is needful to remember, that more often than not, the character with whom Jesus is speaking in the Gospel stories has the greater message. The character is the star; Jesus is the supporting player. As if for an instant in time the predominant character enjoys a mutual responsibility and interdependency with Jesus as to aid the process for the real message or teaching to be heard and seen.

A specific example of expressing mutual responsibility and interdependency is found in the story of the woman at the well, sometimes referred to as the story of the Samaritan or the Syrophoenician woman. A great benefit about the related event is that, to Jesus, woman was no less than any man. This is the longest record in Scripture of conversations he had with a woman; this spurns ancient taboos. Yet so often biases destroy the message as Jesus is manipulated through interpretations to be the dominant character rather than seen as a supporting actor. She lived in Samaria. She was surprised that Jesus would speak to her, especially at the noon hour. To draw water from the town's source was woman's work pure and simple; it was considered beneath the dignity of a man to be seen at the well to obtain water for household consumption.

Furthermore, the drawing of water was a high social feminine function in every village. But it was not done at high noon; the cool of the evening/late afternoon was the ideal time. It was not the practice for this woman to be with the other village women. She was socially unacceptable to her Samaritan neighbours. It is because of this social ostracization that this woman has been dubbed as one of dubious character within the community. Treating her like a person of value, Jesus asked her for a drink. In short, he accepted her. The assumption has been made through history that she was a polygamist or perhaps even a prostitute, that she indirectly received the condemnation of her society. Note, Jesus never reveals the why of her unacceptability. Note, Jesus never judges, corrects, or condemns her.

Consider, that her first husband died of old age since she was given in marriage to this elder as payment for her family's outstanding debt. This was the normal and appropriate behaviour of her era. Her second husband, a soldier killed in battle; the third and fourth husbands could be again logically and reasonably explained. The fifth husband, even if it is common-law, is a relationship by which she has security and is freed from a worse existence. So she returned to the village with the gift, the opportunity for all the people to receive "living water"—redemption.

Obviously the "respectable" were amazed at her message; the populace came out to meet him; they enticed him to stay and he did, for two days. She became the window through which people entered the Godhead as the window of Julian's cell enabled her to enter the lives of the villagers who asked for guidance. This Samaritan woman exemplifies a position all personkind can attain. She teaches that all of us within our society are required to practice mutual responsibility and interdependence. This accomplishment has not been repeated by any other woman or man in our history.

A second reread of another Scripture passage about a socially prominent woman, also brushed aside by androcentric thought, is recorded by Matthew (27:19–20). While Pilate is seated on the judicial bench, he received

49

a message from his wife about the just man, Jesus, who appears before him. But for the insistence of Matthew's recording, the account of this heroine would have been dismissed from history just as easily as her husband could have dismissed her message by the wave of his hand. The significance here is that we may come to realize that there are numerous connecting strands in Scripture that lead to a renewed enlightenment. The incident, only reported in Matthew's Gospel, is striking.

Obviously, for Matthew, the event reported is so important that it must not be lost; and yet the event does not play any outstanding role as far as the actual trial is concerned. The Gospel would flow in its usual way even if verses 19 and 20 had been lost through centuries of copying his work. If you read this chapter to verse 18 and omit the next two verses and reading again the story from verse 21, nothing is lost to the import of the story nor to its outcome. The verses would not be missed. The character of this incidence tends to suggest that it has a special place in the narrative and it bears a reliability in tradition.

Still we ask the question: Why has this part of the story in Matthew been retained? To answer this query, we need to look behind the scenes of the event and attempt to understand the following: Why was Pilate's wife there in Judea? What significance is there in dreams? And who is the person, Pilate's wife? In responding to this interrogation, we may only find conjecture, or we may simply raise other questions, which in turn will attract some concern to the person known as Pilate's wife. In short, we wish to know more about the "heroine" of a certain Friday in the springtime of approximately A.D. 36.

Legend reports that her name was Claudia Procla. That being true, we can say she was an intelligent, cultured woman whose judgement was trustworthy, a woman of Roman nobility and of some influence. There is a traditional belief that she showed a consuming interest in the Judaistic faith of the people her husband ruled as conqueror. To take this a step further, some sources maintain that finally she became a Christian. But that's getting ahead of the story.

The trial of a political upstart called Jesus is in progress. Pilate receives an urgent message from Claudia, which says, "Have nothing to do with that just man; for I have suffered many things this day in a dream because of him." Her plea is not a credible one. She could well have been compassionate in her concern for Jesus. From selfishness, she could have wanted to discuss Judaism with him as he had with another woman at a certain well. Her probing into Judaism was disturbed by this radical Jew, and it is plausible to think that such an opportunity of having him here must not escape her.

On the other hand, she dreamed a dream and became afraid. That is nothing strange or unusual. Many omens are believed to have preceded a particular disastrous event. Roman folklore is full of related experiences. Calpurnia, as an example, had a similar dream regarding Julius Caesar. Dreams, too, in the Matthean account are seen as messages from God; Matthew's account of Jesus' birth in chapters 1 and 2 are pitted with dreams; elaborate messages from God are claimed to have been experienced by Jacob, one of Jesus' ancestors.

Let us consider Claudia, a noble Roman woman, wife of Pilate, included in Matthew's account of the trial of Jesus, from a slightly different perspective. We know, from historical sources, that the Roman Senate permitted the wife of a procurator to accompany her husband if he went to a fairly peaceful land. Here in Judea, Claudia was interested, or had become interested, since her arrival, in Judaism. It is not unreasonable to accept the premise that rumors of Jesus and his works had reached the governor's palace; and still it is not too difficult to believe that she may have seen and heard Jesus in the streets of Jerusalem. Could she have been moved by his nobility and compassion?

Add to that, the probability that she was privy to knowledge about Emporer Tiberius's anger against any procurator who coerced the innocent—and we have ground enough for a nightmare, never mind "a dream." Perhaps she feared for her husband's continuance in office. Or is it only that Claudia Procla had the insight of a kind-hearted woman, and she was trying to stop the action of her husband's headlong callousness? We do not know. We come back to Matthew's persistence in including verses 19 and 20, which no other Gospel writer has done.

It seems that as he is telling the story of the trial, this particular account will be related as a memorial to her. Claudia an intelligent, cultured woman investigating Judaism, seeing and hearing Jesus, and later becoming a Christian, wanted earnestly to have a stay of execution. Pilate could only bring himself to the point declaring his innocence. He feared the loss of his job. As it was, he lost it anyway. The opportunity to talk with Jesus and discuss theology may have come Claudia's way. She could have gained, by that eventuality, an even more prominent a place than that which Matthew seems to give to her.

It has been illustrated that the challenges from Julian's "showings" direct us to a renewed vision of the Godhead and of Scripture. If the previous two references have jolted us into granting a recognition where one was not expected, consider another reference. Rahab, the harlot of Jericho, has been credited with collaborating with Joshua resulting in the downfall of Jericho; through her efforts victory was realized by the ancient peoples (the Chosen Ones—the Jewish nation). But the end of the story is not as forcefully acclaimed.

The armies at Jericho were preventing the Jewish people from continuing their journey from slavery into the land promised to them during Abraham's lifetime. Joshua sent spies to reconnoitre the situation. Why they went to the local house of promiscuity we can only imagine; however, they stayed at Rahab's. She proved to be knowledgeable and conversant about Jewish history and teachings. The spies were discovered; she hid them, and then misguided the searchers. Before aiding the spies' escape from the city, she bargained that at the time of battle, she and her family would be spared. Agreement was reached. The signal that Joshua's invaders honoured was a scarlet cloth tied to the post outside her house, and seeing this marker, they would pass by. All went according to plan. Joshua spared Rahab and her father's household.

Often that is regarded as the conclusion of the episode. Regardless of her business, regardless of her subterfuge, regardless of the escape that she planned and subsequent to that negotiated her freedom, regardless of the Holy Law of Judaism, Rahab was given a most honourable reward beyond the terms of the initial agreement. She was ultimately received into Israel; she became mutually acceptable to the nation. There is documentation that she was married under Jewish law and custom and furthermore that "her descendants dwell in Israel to this day."

The Gentile, heathen Rahab was the agent through which a nomadic Chosen Nation entered the Promised Land; Israel gained freedom. This is a near unmentionable example of equality and interdependence. It is difficult to believe that in our society the daily routine of the workplace and our neighbourhood living fails to express such equality. It is this very discovery that Julian's Sophia-Wisdom desires us to recognize. There is value, dignity, and equality to be found in each individual, and such qualities must not be eradicated by the action and lifestyle of any one person regardless of status, authority, and power by virtue of position or office.

There are many happenings told in the Scriptures that need to be subjected to a rereading and that will on their own merit provide an added richness to the Christian spectrum. Seeing various women in starring roles and seeing them as agents of vital messages serves to question today's Christian community activity. So much activity continues without question, adhering to specific interpretation, and using narrow vision based on androcentric and misogynistic idealism. Fiorenza's analysis is helpful here.[1] These women of "sacred stories" have shown that women can and do bring renewed hope to all personkind. The harassed who have suffered gender segregation, who have been devalued by reason of their femininity, now can receive dignity and enjoy allegiance with God. Those who were contained by society as "outcasts" and who were marginalized cry out again for recognition as they have discovered that they have the equal right to belong in community. These stars come together in a discipleship as equals with all other disciples and they share life with God. For they are novas in our history announcing *shalom,* for us they are beacons indicating and directing that Sophia-Wisdom of God is still much alive to us and is available for partnership in our activity.

To merely write these things and to give the intellectual nod of assent is to ascend only to a patronizing attitude. We need to learn these statements by enforcing practice of the messages. We need to learn first to present the plausible Godhead to our society for the benefit of personkind. The ritual, ceremony, and rhetoric of our worship should enable the I AM WHO I AM to enter the lives of the worshippers. Then the people may well discover that the vehicle of worship allows them to learn more about the God who loves them and they may come to realize that God does respect the decisions that people have made. We are made in the image of God, yet more often we do not portray that we are a part of the Essence, a part of the Divinity.

The Church also teaches most emphatically the omnipresence of God; again then, every effort should secure equality and interdependence as attainable goals to be accepted and embraced. There is no question in this author's mind concerning the truth and validity of Julian's teachings, as well as what has been previously stated in this chapter, so let us "get on with our mission" as God's community on earth. Many people may well have a desire to rescind responsibility for their well-being, reserving it to only a powerful Father figure regarded with an unquestioning submission, but that is not what the Church is about.

The Church, the gathered community of God, is charged with the dedicated responsibility for the spiritual growth of and catering to those who have found sanctuary in the old ways. But there is another task, a task truer to the charge, a task that exceeds the importance of a caterer. The Church, too, must be a place for all individuals to rethink, to rediscover one's relationship with Creator, Redeemer, Nurturer, Comforter. The Church must renew itself to become the place where personkind may even bring seemingly heretical thoughts into its offertory. Why? Because, all through the story of Scripture, it is in the place and purpose of common prayer that the Godhead has reacted and enacted with Her people for the benefit of all creation. Then, perhaps, relationships would be renewed, fear of ethereal feudalism be dispelled, restraints of gender be disintegrated, and harmony and communion-union be achieved.

The life, teachings, and "showings" of Julian plunge us into many other lessons. This highly intelligent lady of Norwich is a person of great sensitivity whose experience shows us in this part of the twentieth century that the Church has not dealt effectively, as it has the capabilities to do, with the concepts of God our Mother or Sophia-Wisdom. Her kaleidoscope imagery allows us to comprehend her understanding of the human conditions and possibility within those conditions for growth into equality, respect, and dignity of personkind. Julian has so much to teach us, and these lessons can be meted out through the Church into every part of our society.

Two dramatic and traumatic concerns into which we still are slow to invade are: the issue of abortion and the intentional or unintentional actions of those holding power and authority in the workplace to misuse, manipulate, and marginalize others.

Before we make an attempt to learn more from the works of Julian regarding these two interfretted concerns, a word or two needs to be stated about our terminology. Expressions exist in everyday speech as: "feminist theology," "feminist movement," "woman-church," "it's my body, I'm in charge of it." These can be seen as negative and defeatist terms. This author emphatically acknowledges that these word choices came into existence because of frustration, anxiousness, and violence experienced both mentally and physically by women. Further, that an unyielding determination to be heard became so unimaginably powerful that the "new vocabulary" was sensed as unquestionably necessary; and for a specific time and place, that was probably quite true. But the continued use of this phraseology can lead very quickly to ostracization and segregation within society. There is proof of that having taken place already.

Since we do not desire to be guilty of contributing to drawing these battle lines, such misanthropic and egotistic word patterns hopefully will not appear. To cause additional confrontation surrounding similar word choices would be counterproductive to our learning. Indeed, more wounds would be inflicted, prolonging a healing process that is already long overdue. Our lesson from Julian is to bring "mankind" into "personkind"; it is to have us graduate into a living community in which interwovenness, interdependence, equality, and dignity is experienced through the integration of two perspectives. These perspectives—the feminine and the masculine—are identified with dignity and accepted with equality. This is the theology exhibited by belief (doctrine) in God our Mother and Sophia-Wisdom.

An issue that has become one of the most sensitive and electrifying is that concerning abortion. The Church, to give leadership and to expound teaching here, must do so with the wisdom of the prophet mixed with the compassion of the nurturer. As we meet the person confronted with the option of abortion, we do well to remember that judgmental decision making does nothing to serve the future well-being of that particular person. To meet the person where she is mentally and spiritually is paramount to her well-being in contrast to imposing concepts on her that can only be identified with where we expect her to be mentally and spiritually. It is not only the Church that has been ineffective in wrestling with this issue, but the whole of our social infrastructure is baffled by the copious compilations of reactions arising from both the emotional and the intellectual aspects. Church and state are pathetic in ministering to all personkind faced with the possibility of using abortion practices.

There are certain events that condition the abortion decision. Causation can complicate the facilitation of more rational response. Yet answers are demanded, and subsequent actions seem to be casuistic choices among many solutions. For instance, the rape victim is in need of extensive support, compassion, and nurturing rather than becoming the subject of judgmental attitudes exhibited by many of society's agencies and law-enforcement associations. The inflicting of such additional violent traumas upon an individual are events that should not be allowed to compound the other devastating issue. When rape or nonrape are conditions for which one considers abortion, probably decisions may not be made for the same reason. Also, are we to subject the person to an abortion decision using the same problem-solving models when rape was committed within marriage? "To do the wifely duty only, or to fulfill the wifely function only" is rape. How is the decision to abort the pregnancy arrived at within that lifestyle?

Third, the abortion, for whatever reason, of nonwhites can be complicated within the racist issue; and so, abortion becomes the tool of an even more sinister socially tolerated practice. Recall, where any part of white-dominated society rules, for any person living in that community, then any definitive action can be translated as a racist act. Therefore rules determining a decision of abortion can be heard as the accusation toward white people, even white female people, as supporting the status of the traditional white-male hierarchy. We continue to pose the question, whatever became of personkind? The subject matter of these three mentioned issues is worthy of its own treatise. Our purpose in this lesson is to discover our relationship as a part of personkind with the "uncomplicated" and "usual conditioned" pregnancy for which abortion is requested.

Abortion becomes an issue when completion of term is not desired, not wanted, or considered to be appropriate. Some examples of the most common scenarios presenting pregnancy/abortion discussions follow:[2]

1. A high school student who is eighteen years of age has become pregnant. After her pregnancy test proved positive, she recounted that "it" is not wanted. She is not ready for "it"; she is not ready to be a mother. Next year is her last year in high school; she cannot afford to have any restrictions imposed on the goal of completing her graduation from school. The decision to have an abortion is weighted by the fact that her needs are in conflict. Other eighteen-year-old women may see this as an opportunity for an escape and enter the marital state, thereby achieving freedom from their own home life. However, the restrictions imposed on life goals, for example the immediate educational achievements, become too enormous to accept when coupled with marriage and another home.

2. A woman in her midtwenties is two months pregnant with her second child. She is a Roman Catholic with

a strong moral drive, which determines that a decision to have an abortion is one of some urgency. For her the absence of acceptance of legal abortion raises a great moral conflict; and there is an important conflict between her own self-satisfaction and her self-sacrifice to ensure protection and care for another dependent. A second child contrary to medical advice, she is convinced, would strain the family financially and emotionally. She does not want to be tied down any more than she is currently. So, this woman intellectualizes by justifying her anticipated emotional distress over the need to care for husband and child and an additional child.

3. A musician is in her midthirties and enjoys an independent life, enabling her to concentrate on her work. This person is fairly strong-willed, in control, rational, and objective. Through her romantic experiences, she learned about the extent of her naïveté and idealism. The conflicts she encounters range from concerns over acceptance of her by her lover, to the need for more support than she thought was available. Philosophically, she argued about abortion: to have children in ideal conditions is the only reason to add to the world's population; and her strong desire to have a child. The final decision was to abort, since there seemed to be an imbalance between handling the pregnancy and retaining a confidence in her work.

The validity of all arguments incorporates the psychological sphere, a pragmatism concerning survival, the moral issues regarding the loss of self-respect and an honest desire to become a mother. But, at the same time, from all arguments presented, what is basically common to every situation centres on the self "in the here and now." The question that was never asked, nor was there any indication of thought given to the concept is, Is the fetus a person? There are other cognitive concerns too that were seemingly ignored: Is the fetus a person as I am a person? Is the fetus a part of the great I AM WHO I AM? What of the interdependency between mother, father, and fetus?

The medical and legal professions attempt to rule and regulate the abortion issue ad nauseam. The point here is not to delve into such debates and become caught in the exercise of defining wounds of verbiage. That has been detailed very efficiently by others to themselves, but there are some observations that need to be specifically noted.[3] Many attempt to render agreement that abortion is equal to killing, or that it is merely the removal of an object that is a live organism. The debate over the status of the fetus is one in which the resolve is lost because the personalities on either side fail to learn the message employed in the very word "person." So sugary rhetoric is used up to consider whether the fetus is human or person, and if so, then how can a person be part of another person?

The argument continues: if that is true, then the one person must be less of a person than the other; and, after all, the fetus really cannot be a person because it is not rational. Discussions advance nowhere on this vicious circular treadmill, which erroneously charges the adrenalin flow until some believe that something of significance is being fathomed. But these professionals have been duped by their own words. Another interjection into these talks contemplates the differences of the fetus according to: size, development, dependency, and mobility. Suddenly the abortion argument tests the moral relevancy of "killing" based on those very differences.

We pause to take special note here, that although "person" was given some consideration, usually any discussion of this subject is quick to abandon the argument for the easier and already resolved legal and medical regulation. The topic then becomes one of choosing whether the argument fits the parameters of other definitions. Yet "Is the fetus a person?"—is the question that remains unanswered.

To our legal, medical expertise, we can add the philosopher and the theologian. This author is not convinced that the abortion question is one of theology; in fact, with all certainty this author contends strongly that there is no theological focus in this debate, nor should there be. The contention surrounds the question of fetus vis-à-vis person; it is because the issue of personkind has a definitive and specific basis in theology that the theologian foolishly allows his or her involvement in this debate. Too, there is a sense within society of the appropriateness that the theologian should be involved, albeit he or she is not taken too, too seriously. It is impossible, or at least, extremely difficult to legislate (morality) ethics. Laws restricting abortion practices, members of the legal profession accurately maintain are unenforceable. These professionals, as mirrors of our society, come to realize that none of the arguments against abortion grow from religious or theological concepts.

Rather what is heard again and again results from very simple pragmatic and survival statements: "I don't want to be a mother"; "the child will be an imposition"; "we have to get a goodly amount of money, and a large enough house, and a car first"; "my career is too important"; and "I'll lose my self-respect." Following those thought processes then, discussions turn irrevocably to the (moral) ethic ideal. If life is sacred in the abortion clinic, why not also on the battlefield? It is found that liberalism and freedom of choice must be justified. From that stance is developed "the pro-life" and the "pro-choice" poles. Having absorbed much energy and time, the analysis of our deliberations to this point supplies us with a truth we already know: depending with which camp one agrees—someone is right, and the other is wrong. Abortion is a decision from an opinion (at best), and all opinions are equal.

What has been resolved of the primary and real issue? Nothing! The question remains unanswered, "Is the fetus a person?" Without the answer, men and women will continue to be judgmental and focus blame that will have further unimaginable, devastating results. Compassion for one's self can no longer be ignored. Compassion is a feeling. Compassion is supporting others and caring for others, so that others can avoid and/or can tolerate suffering. We have compassion for strangers and friends; and we care more deeply for our children; and a lover cares more about life than does a non-lover. These ideals bring us back to that question which is so aggravating. "Is the fetus a person?"

Person encapsulates the whole essence of being, and it is that which Julian of Norwich dictates we learn through her writings. The aggravation is caused because we are unable to rid ourselves of that specific query that needs a solution. The lesson Julian asks us to learn includes giving more consideration to other fundamental principles: Is it that person designates the whole reality of creation? Is it that person has us sharing in the nature of the I AM WHO I AM? Is it that person determines that we are to enjoy equality and interdependence? Is one fetus or person unequal to another? Is it not that relationships develop through interdependency? Is not that the quality of maturity is measured by society itself by how well one interacts with another?

The second issue—the intentional or unintentional actions of those holding power and authority in the work place to misuse, manipulate, and marginalize others—is born out of a depreciation of who we are.[4] Correction of this condition, or even a visual turnaround of this predicament, has received little constant attention throughout society. Even leadership emitted from the Church regarding this serious matter has been very poor. Some counter that Church leadership to rid ourselves of this situation is becoming stronger; those people certainly have a right to their opinion. But current practices seem to support the premise that little attention has been constantly directed into that sphere of our living. That One, Holy, Catholic, and Apostolic institution surely is that part of society in which and from which definite and strong leadership is expected. At least, from the day of Julian, the Church should have been heard relentlessly proclaiming teachings of equality, value, and dignity for personkind. We not only have not learned our lessons well, but seemingly we have heard a befuddled account of the "showings" of the anchoress of Norwich.

There are chauvinists among us. Points of view that demonstrate patriarchal, androcentric, misogynist convictions would conclude that since sexual differences are innate and natural, therefore it is anticipated that women are completely inferior to men. For people who hold such points of view, it is as though sex were the premise from which value, equality, dignity, and personhood are derived. In fact, these persons would contend further that interdependency and being a part of the very essence of the I AM WHO I AM depends upon maleness. To initiate, nurture and promote a turnabout in attitude and lifestyle, we must be very careful not to commit the other and equally wrong concept of the unisexual. That is, women are not inferior, but the superior ones and that sexual differences are unnatural. Both conclusions are wrong. Both premises become foiled in debate; both lose sight of the lesson, which is to arrive in understanding and acceptance that man and woman are persons equally created, nurtured, redeemed, and cared for.

Society has acquired such paranoia that it is difficult to speak and act uninhibitedly in the marketplace. Why? Because we have not heard nor learned our lessons. Why? One reason is that men and women fail to view themselves as persons having an innate right of dignity, respect, interdependence, and equality. Never before has there been so much confusion about how to accept women in the working place. Society has become so conditioned into normalizing boxed structures. These structures have additional built-in features, which give concessions to "for men only" conditions.

Just as our concept of God can be fixed by boxed-in androcentric power trips, so our mind sets regarding the marketplace can be fixed on male domination. Letting God out of the box is permitting personkind's experience of God to be utilized for one's personal growth and development, which, in turn, can be greatly beneficial to all. So opening the boxed-in in the marketplace can allow the attainment of each person's self-realization to become an integral factor of society's well-being. It is an acceptance of reality to become fully aware that woman has a legitimate drive toward self-actualization, and that this is not to be seen as a strange or peculiar act of fate or a social machination of twentieth-century modernism. We are to discover that the interwoven web of society will become stronger through the working out and practice of interdependency. A nurturing and a caring society creates patterns of life so beneficial to society itself that the quality of daily life will surpass the expectations of our imaginations. Freedom is the reward. Freedom from:

1. The great tension and confusion of our daily existence. Our marketplaces will no longer be experiences of imprisonment through confusion and paranoias concerning what is the appropriate behaviour or word in any given situation. Our domestic life will cease to be controlled by the pressure release valves from which stored-up emotions and attitudes are blasted upon the innocent. Never before in society has it become so important to get the rules of the marketplace correctly. How extreme we have become in the devaluation of personkind is evident by reactions of third parties. The familiar and friendly word, and the comraderie of the purely innocent touch, is immediately interpreted by a third party through judgmental assumptions as a violation of human rights or as incorrect conduct or as a particular harassment.

That atmosphere is so volatile that undocumented views by third parties are accepted without an investigation concerning the development. Judgmental attitudes come out of need for revenge for past events involving either individual or jealousy by a third party of those involved in the present event. Once the accusation is voiced, not one life, but several lives are destroyed and the potential of one individual is decimated. Freedom from all this is gained in learning the lesson of the value of personkind and the value we hold for ourselves.

2. The embarrassments and judgment calls when assessing where one is in life; freedom for a person to substantiate his or her professional viewpoint; freedom from

all anxiety that the professional will not be accepted as a valued member of the specific discipline, freedom from the affliction of degradation by others because of gender (or disability). For example, the single, female parent who educated herself through law school, graduated cum laude, but continues to suffer society's patriarchal and misogynistic status quo as employment opportunities become scarce by reason of gender. The eventuality of being retained by a law firm does not end the devaluation of this person. The disregard for interdependency finds this woman lawyer confronting the magistrate in his chambers because he did not allow her to express herself before in court. That magistrate, on his own recognisance only, recognized the wisdom, the perspective, the knowledge she possessed was inadequate to uphold the integrity and reverence for democratic principles.

Professionals within their associations are no different from other elements of society; there are no secure ivory towers where anyone is to discern "person." Yet, it is reasonable to assume that this should not be a situation in our Christian communities. The Church absolutely, and the professionals certainly, need to take the leadership that proclaims and exemplifies personkind's interdependency and dignity. The aim, method, and conclusion of this lesson is to accept with confidence the fact that the ability and experience gained by another are the credentials by which that person attains growth development and achieves full potential.

A further lesson we receive from Julian's "showings" concerns the use of position and status by which we have restrained personkind. Church and society could dominate leadership by allowing self-actualization of the individual to become a norm. Self-actualization is a technical term. This is a basic need of every person; it does not pertain or belong only to the work-place, nor to masculine superiority. Self-actualization means becoming all that one is capable of becoming. No role of one partner involves the right or authority to dominate another, and thereby prevent or suppress the upswelling of that basic need in the other partner—regardless of condition or situation. Self-actualization allows a person to choose tasks, opportunities that they like, and permits them to enjoy the satisfaction of accomplishing those tasks. This challenges the concepts of equality, and the value of personkind. It challenges the known concept that the whole person is activated in the work-place; that a person has a direct and indirect relational reaction toward every other person in the work-place, e.g., skills, abilities, and creativity are in a direct relation to the marketplace.

But, too, there is the indirect relation where the status of home life and lifestyle profoundly affects productivity. People are generally treated differently because of these tangible and intangible factors, and rightly so. The separate personality has a right to grow toward potentialities and to pursue, uninhibitedly, self-fulfillment within the bounds of responsibility. This can mean a change or shift in who is to work in the marketplace because of a reevaluation of these bounds. It is here that we need to learn our lessons. Too often, the intrinsic factors are completely ignored, so much so that the other members of a household are conveniently considered as outside of the decision-making process, even the decisions that result in the relocation of all family members. There can be, and appropriately so, significant concern about impending transfers from one work-place to another area. This can have a traumatic effect.

This can be seen as a suppression of the partner's self-actualization and potential employment. Where self-actualization is beginning to be realized through experience by one partner and decision to relocate by the other without due consideration of the other's life existence can be comprehended as devaluing the importance of the other. By these subsequent events, it could be logically presumed that the predominant employment factor has been assumed as residing in the male member. Why? Does this not maintain and dictate that the lesser employment is that of the female member? Is this not declaring that the self-actualization is accountable only by male-dominant employment? Should there be no review regarding the family work ethic? From time to time, can there not be a review of roles within the family structure? A review of this nature may well heighten self-actualization and reveal a discovery of one's desire to shift roles free from peer ridicule.

Is it dignified, helpful, equally and mutually responsible for one's satisfaction to be uprooted, terminated because indifferent circumstances dictate? Perhaps the male member would desire to have an extended sabbatical from the stereotype of work place existence and perhaps the female member wishes to enjoy a different role filled with the satisfaction of accomplishment in another sphere. Our male-dominant society has much ammunition to suggest that such employment toleration would spell disaster to our life and economy. That simply is not true nor is it believable. If we accept "person," if we work at interdependence, if we believe the concepts of equality, self-actualization, and dignity, then we dare not lay claim to such an item merely as gender orientation. This discussion has now reached the very heart of our society. It is the individual who must confront and resolve these basic and fundamental principles of our very nature. We need to learn our lessons; this Lady of Norwich has more to say to the Church today, as well as to each of us in our living.

Notes

1. Elisabeth Schussler Fiorenza, *In Memory of Her* (New York: Crossroads Publishing, 1990) 133–36.

2. Carol Gilligan, *In a Different Voice* (Cambridge: Harvard University Press, 1982).

3. Peter Kreeft, *The Unaborted Socrates* (Illinois: University Press, Downers Grove, 1983).

4. "Unintentional actions" recognizes the fact that everyone has been so programmed by the past that no one remains untouched by androcentric and misogynistic influences.

Postscript

The cell of Norwich is silent;
And has been for only too long a time.
Julian challenges me—
To awaken the silence.
There is a comradeship to share—with Julian
there is a perception—a discovery of God
for all to enter.
To weave the interwovenness of God
and live together;
for each is a thread that brings
their own interdependency
of understanding, hope, actualization,
love and dignity.
For each person is a thread that builds
and strengthens the other.
The lessons from the anchoress
are precious.
Lead us on, Julian,
so we can celebrate all life
prayers
laughter
work
worship
together, in reverence and respect
for each of personkind.

Appendixes

Appendix A
A Concept of "Wisdom" (Sophia)

It is quite easy to become confused during any discussion regarding Wisdom. Jewish and Christian scholars have shared this experience for centuries. We must be, therefore, as meticulous and as explicit as our abilities allow as we search the collection of Holy Writ designated in the Scriptures as the Wisdom literature. The place given to Wisdom literature is as all-encompassing in our history as Wisdom is baffling to the textual critics. Topics permeated by Wisdom reach into every aspect of society, religious community, and administrations of justice and community affairs.

In addition to the conflagration come the related definitions inferred by the Hebraic words we so easily translate as "wisdom." *Hokinah* and *Hakamin* do give specific meanings to wisdom and can invoke other meanings in particular relationships. The concepts that are of concern here, are the significant relationships wisdom holds for the Ancient Peoples. Through certain situations and under certain ideas, wisdom was known as a divine personification and was awarded a position within the Omnipresence, Omnipotence, and Omniscience of the Godhead. The use of pronouns She/He does not necessarily grant gender to God, but provided a perspective, a personality, a space, a hypostasis to be recognized in the nature of the Godhead. Aside from passages in Wisdom of Solomon, other Wisdom literature (Proverbs 8 and Sirach 24 are examples) give place and divinity to Sophia-Wisdom. Similar to the Julian imagery of interwovenness, Sophia is pictured as surrounding and exploring the whole creation, an activity that was traditionally reserved for and attributed to God the Father. The concept here describes Her (Sophia-Wisdom) as uniquely and intricately related to all creation. She is God's expression and activity. She is God.

Additionally, there is a resistance toward making companions of those segments of Wisdom literature and New Testament writings. Scholars have thought it necessary, for a variety of reasons, to follow the lines of the textual critics sometimes by relentlessly treating them in isolation. Scholars, also, have implied that Wisdom is a part of the Second Person of the Trinity. Yet, through the reading of Wisdom passages (and from the showings of Julian of Norwich, and also through the deliberations of other scholars such as Oesterley), there is a growing perception that Sophia-Wisdom is a personification within the very nature and essence of the Godhead.

Also, Julian seems to enjoy a flirtation in placing Wisdom as dwelling within and as finding expression within the I AM WHO I AM. This is most enriching. Freedom to determine a relationship with God that is not limited by the dictates of man-made doctrinal structures. It allows the expression of God as She/He is experienced and seen in creation to be verbalized and taken as a legitimate belief, and provides the way for a broader and more secure theology of God. This theology enables a stronger vehicle to be used for the communication of the omnipresence, omniscience, and omnipotence of God Herself.

Appendix B
Translation of "The Lord and the Servant" Parable

In this translation I have attempted to maintain a respectable integrity and faithfulness to the text. In some parts, the reader may find herself/himself struggling a little with the translation as it appears to err on the side of being too literal. This is done purposefully. I have not paraphrased, or editorialized the text nor have I assumed what Julian was trying to say. I leave such interpretation to the reader; I believe the reader must be permitted the luxury of gaining a more personal insight from the parable than that expressed by anyone else. On the occasional times I have felt it necessary to give an interpretation, I have done so by expressing my understanding of Julian using *italics* and in brackets [. . .], immediately following the specific translated portion of the text.

Now, to the parable of "The Lord and The Servant" written by Julian of Norwich in Chapter 51, Revelation 14 of her showings as recorded in the longer version.

The Lord and the Servant

And then
our courteous lord answered in showing [full] mysteriously and
    symbolically by a wonderful example of a lord who had a
    servant,
and gave me sight to understand both.
Which sight was shown doubly [*a twofold expression*] in the
    lord,
and the sight was shown doubly [*a twofold expression*] in the
    servant.
That one matter was shown spiritual in the likeness of a body
    [*physical body*].
Thus for the first I saw two persons in body [*physical body*]
likeness, that is to say a lord and a servant;
and therewith [*meanwhile*] god gave spiritual understanding.
The lord sat solemnly in rest and in peace [*silence*].
The servant being the case [*stood*]
before his lord, reverently ready to do his lord's will.
The lord looks upon his servant with full love and sweetly with
humility [*submissively*].
He sends him in
to a certain place to do
his will.
The servant not only goes,
but suddenly
he departs [*launches out*]
and runs in great haste
for the love to do his lord's will.
And immediately he fell in a valley [*precipice*]
and takes injuries greatly sorrow [*painful*];
and then he groans and moans
and rolling [*tosses about*]
and twists,
but he may not rise nor

help himself in [any] manner of way.
And of all this the most mischief
that I saw he was in feeling no comfort,
for he could not turn his face
to the extent of looking upon [looking up] on his loving lord,
who was full [very] near,
in whom is full comfort;
but as a man that was full [very] feeble and unwise for the
  time [lacking in wisdom],
he attended to his feeling and
enduring in sorrow,
in which sorrow he suffered seven great pains.
The first was the hard bruising
that he took in his falling,
which was to him [gave to him] much pain.
The second was the abundance [weight] of his body.
The third was the feebleness that followed these two.
The fourth was that his reason was blinded [stunned] and
  bewildered
in his mind so to such a degree that
he had almost forgotten his own love.
The fifth was that he might not rise.
The sixth was pain most marvellous [astonishing] to me,
and that he was laying alone.
I looked all about and beheld,
and feared that not near
not high
not low
I saw [did I see] no help to him.
The seventh was that the place which he lay in was long, hard
  and
grievous [oppressive].
I marvelled [was astonished]
how this servant might thus humbly [submissively]
suffer all this sorrow;
And I beheld with clearly [clarity] to know
if I could perceive in him one [any]

imperfection, or if the lord should assign in him one manner
    of blame;
Truly there was none seen, for only his good will and his great
    desire caused his falling.
He was as unreluctant and as good inwardly as he was when
    he being the case [*stood upright*] before his lord,
ready to do his will.
And exactly thus
continually his loving lord
full tenderly beholds him;
And now with a double [*a twofold expression*] expression,
one outward, full humility [*submissively*]
and mildly with great compassion
and disposed to mercy [*affection*],
Another inward,
more spiritual,
and this was shown with a
leading of my understanding into the lord,
in restoring which I saw
him
highly enjoying for the reverently resting
and nobleness that
he will and
shall bring
his servant to
by his plenteous grace.
And this was that other showing.
And now was my understanding
led again to the first, keeping
both in mind.
Than said the courteous lord
in his meaning:
        ["] Lo, my beloved
servant what harm and disease [*dis-ease* or *unease*] he had
    taken in my service for my love,
yes, and for his good will.
        Is it not reason that I reward

80

him for his fear and his dread,
his hurt and his maimed [*bodily injury*], and all his sorrow?
  And not only this,
but falling to me [*does it not fall to me*] to give him a gift
more reverently than his own
health should have been?
  Otherwise me thinks I did him no grace. ["]
And in this an inward spiritual
showing of the lord's meaning descended into my soul,
in which I saw that it behooves [*it is a necessity*]
to be standing [*to show* or *to reveal*]
his great goodness and his own reverence, that his dear worthy
  [*delightful*] servant,
which he loved so much
should be highly and blessfully [*joyously*]
rewarded without end above all that he should have—if he had
  not fallen,
yes, and so
that his falling and all his sorrow that he has taken there shall
  be
turned into the high surpassing
reverence and
endless blessing [*joy*].
At this point the showing of the example vanished,
and our good lord led my understanding
in sight
and in showing of the revelation
to the end.
But notwithstanding all this
forthleading [*fore knowledge*] the astounding example
never went from me;
for me, [I], thought
it was given me for an answer to my desire.
yet, could I not take [*find*] there in full understanding
to me eyes in that time.
For the servant, that was shown for Adam
as I shall say,

81

I saw many diverse properties [*characteristics*]
that might by no manner
be directed singularly [*only*] to Adam,
and so in that time I stood [*stayed*] labouring in three
      knowings,
for the full understanding of this astonishing example was not
      given me at that time.
In which mysterious example of secrets [*essential properties* or
      contemplative knowledge] of the revelation
be yet much hidden;
and notwithstanding this I saw
and understood
that every showing is full of secrets [*essential properties* or
      contemplative knowledge]
and therefore it behooves me now to tell three properties
      [*characteristics*]
which I am somewhat eased.
The first is the beginning of teaching that I
understood there [*at*] the same time.
The second is the inward learning that I have understood there,
with grief and sorrow.
The third is all the whole revelation
from the beginning to the end
which our lord god of his goodness brings
oftentimes, freely
to the sight of my understanding.
And these three be as so one to my understanding,
that I cannot nor may depart from them.
And by these three as one I have teaching whereby alas
I am to believe
and trust in our lord god,
that of the same goodness that he
showed it
and for the same end,
exactly so
of the same goodness and for the same end
he shall declare it to

us when it is his will.
For twenty years, after the time of the showing save three
      months
I had teaching inwardly
as I shall say [*tell*]:
it longs [*yearns*]
to take heed to all the properties [*details*]
and conditions that were shown in the example,
though the thought that it be mysterious and indifferent to
      sight.
I consent willingly with great
desire,
seeing inwardly clearly
all points
and the properties [*details*] that were
shown in the same time,
as to such a degree
my wit and understanding
will serve,
beginning my beholding [*viewing*]
at the lord and at the servant,
at the manner and
the place the lord sits,
and the colour of his disguise [*clothing*] and the manner of
      shape,
and his expression
without and his nobleness
and his goodness within;
and the manner of the standing of the servant,
the place and how,
he stands and his manner of disguise [*clothing*],—
the colour and shape,
his outward behaviour and his inward goodness and
      unreluctancy.
The lord that sat solemnly in rest and peace [*silence*],
I understand he is god.
The servant that stood before him,

I understand that he was shown
for [*to resemble* or *to be* or *to symbolically be*] Adam,
that is to say one man was shown
at that time and his falling
to make there by to be understood how god
beholds all man [*mankind*]
and his falling.
For in the sight of god
all man
is one man
and one man
is all man.
This man was hurt in his might and made full feeble,
and he was bewildered in his understanding
for he was turned
from the beholding
of his lord,
but his will was kept
in god's sight.
For his will I saw our lord
commend and approve,
but himself was delayed [*impeded*]
and blinded of knowing of this will. And this is to him great
      sorrow and
grievous disease [*dis-ease* or *unease*];
for neither he sees
clearly his loving lord which
is to him full humble [*submissive*] and mild,
nor he sees truly who himself
is in the sight of his loving lord.
And well I know when these two
be wisely and truly seen
we shall
get rest and peace [*silence*],
here in part and the abundance in the joy
in heaven
by his plenteous grace.

And this was a beginning of teaching
which I saw in the same time,
whereby I might come to know in what
manner he beholds us in our sin.
And than I saw the only pain that blames
and punishes
and our courteous lord
comforts and succours [*supports* or *spiritually aids*],
and even he is to the soul
glad expression,
loving and longing to bring us to
his joy.
The place that the lord sat on was
simply on the earth,
barren [the sense here is—*nude*]
and desert [*deserted*]
alone in the wilderness.
His disguise [*clothing*] was wide [*ample*]
and part of the human body [*and a good fit*]
and full seemly [*visually pleasing*]
as falls to [*becomes*] to a lord.
The colour of the disguise [*clothing*] was blue as azure,
most dignified and fair.
His expression was merciful,
the colour of his face [*countenance*]
was fair brown
while with fulsome
features his eyes were black,
most fair seemingly
showing full of lovely pity [*compassion*],
and within him a high world [*place of refuge*]
long and broad,
all full of endless heavenliness.
The lovely looking that he looked [*regarded*]
his servant continually
and namely
[the sense that at the time of—*even*—] when his falling,

me [*I*] thought it might melt our hearts
for love and break them in two for joy.
This fair looking showed a seemly
mixture which was marvellous to behold.
The one was compassion and pity,
that other joy and blessing [*every joy*].
The joy and blessing [*every joy*]
pass as for the compassion and pity
as heaven is above earth.
The pity was earthy and the joy heavenly.
The compassion and pity of the father
was the falling of Adam, which
is the most loved creature.
The joy and blessing [*every joy*] was the falling of his worthy
     son,
who is equal with the father.
The merciful beholding of his lovely expression
fulfilled all earth,
and descended down with Adam
into hell,
with which persistent pity
Adam was kept from endless death.
And his mercy and pity dwells with
mankind in to the time that
we come arisen in to heaven.
But man is blinded in this life,
and therefore we may not see our
father-god as he is.
And what time that he of his
goodness will show him to man,
he showed him familiar manner [*friendly*] as man,
not withstanding
that I saw truly, we ought to know and believe that the father
     is not man.
But his sitting on the earth,
desert and
barren [*nude*],

86

is this serving as a means [*in common togetherness*]:
he made man's soul to be his own walled city
and his dwelling place which is most pleasing
to him of all his works.
And what time man was fallen into sorrow
and pain, he was not all seemly to
serve that noble office;
and therefore our kind father would have
adorned him no other place
but to sit upon the earth, abiding [*waiting for*]
mankind, which is mixed with earth,
'til what time by his grace
his beloved son had brought again his walled city
into the noble fairness
with his hard labour.
The blueness of the disguise [*clothing*] betokens
his firm belief [*constancy/unchanging*],
the browness of his fair face with the
seeming blackness of the eyes
was most according
to show his completely soberness
the liberalness of his disguise [*clothing*]
which was fair flowing about,
betokens that he has enclosed in him all heavens
and all endless joy
and bliss [*happiness*];
and this was showed in a touch [*in a brief moment*], was where
    I saw
that my understanding was led in to
the lord;
In which I saw him mightily
enjoy [*rejoicing*] for the worthy restoring that he wills and
shall bring his servant to by his plenteous
grace.
And yet I marvelled,—beholding the lord
and the servant
before telling. I saw the lord sitting solemnly,

and the servant standing reverently before

his lord, in which servant is doubly [*with a two-fold expression*]
    understanding [*significant*],

one without,

and another within.

Outward he was clad simply,

as a labourer which was disposed [*readied*] to labour,

and he stood full near the lord, not equal for location [*with*]
    him,

but in a part and that on the left side;

his disguise [*clothing*] was a white tunic,

single

old

all defaced [*lacking* or *defective in use*]

dyed with his body [*aroma*], tight fitting to him and short,

as it were a handful below the knee,

threadbare,

as it should soon be worn

to the extent of it, [*worn out*]

ragged and torn.

And in this I marvelled greatly,

thinking:

this is now an unusual disguise [*clothing*] for

that servant that so highly loved to stand before so worthy a
    lord.

And inward in him was showed

a ground [*fundamental/originally based*] of love,

which love he had—to the lord,

that was ever like to the love that the lord had to him.

The wisdom of the servant saw inwardly that there was one
    thing to do

which should be worthy to the lord;

and the servant for love,

having no reward to himself nor

having nothing that might fall to him [*happen to him*],

hasty deed departed and running

at the sounding [*bidding*] of his lord,

to do that thing which was his will and his worth;
For it seemed by his outward disguise [*clothing*] as he had been
a persevering labourer and a hard labourer of long time.
And by the inward sight that I had
both in the lord and in the servant,
it seemed that he was newed [*newly appointed*],
that is to say new beginning for to labour, which servant was
never sent out before.
There was a treasure in the earth
which the lord loved.
I marvelled and thought what it might be;
I was answered in my understanding:
it is a food [*sustenance*] which is lovesome and pleasing to the
lord.
For I saw the lord sitting as a man
and I saw neither meat or drink
wherewith to serve him.
This was one marvel;
another marvel was that this solemn lord had no servant but
one, and him he sent out.
I looked, thinking what manner labour
it may be that the servant should do.
And then I understood that he should do
the greatest labour and the hardest
labour there is.
He should be a gardener,
digging and making a ditch,
perspiring
turning the earth up and down, and
assure the deepness
and water the plants in time.
And in this he should endure his labours,
and make sweet floods to run
and noble plenteous fruits to
spring [*grow*],
which he should bring before the lord, and serve
them therewith to his liking.

He should never turn again,
till he had prepared this meat dish all ready,
as he knew it liked to the lord;
and then he should take this meat with the drink,
and bear it
full reverently before the lord.
All this time the lord should sit
exactly on the same place,
abiding [*waiting for*] the servant he sent out.
And yet I marvelled from whom the servant came,
for I saw in the lord that
he has within himself endless life
and all manner of goodness, save the treasure that was on
    earth,
and that was grounded [*fundamental/originally based*] with
    the lord in
marvellous deepness of endless love.
But it was not all to his honour till his servant has thus nobly
prepared it and brought it before him in himself present [*in
    his presence*].
Without the lord was exactly nothing but wilderness:
and I understood not all with this example [*parable*].
Therefore I marvelled from where the servant came.
In the servant is comprehended the second person of the trinity,
and in the servant is comprehended Adam, that is to say all
    men.
And therefore when I see the son it means the godhead which
    is equal with the father
and when I see the servant it means Christ's manhood which
    is rightfully Adam.
By the closeness of the servant
is understood the son,
and by the being the case [*standing*] of the left side is
    understood Adam.
The lord is god the father,
the servant is the son Jesu Christ
the holy ghost [*spirit*] is the equal

love which is in them both.
When Adam fell god's son fell;
for the exactly once which was made in heaven,
god's son might not be separate from Adam,
for by Adam I understood all man.
Adam fell from life to death,
in to the valley [*precipice*] of the
wretched world, and after that in to hell.
God's son fell with Adam in to
the valley [*precipice*] of the maiden's womb,
which was the fairest daughter
of Adam,
and that for to excuse Adam from blame in heaven and in
    earth; and mightily he fetched him out of hell. By the
    wisdom and the goodness that was in the servant is
understood god's son
by the poor disguise [*clothing*] as a labourer
being the case [*standing*]
near the left side is understood the manhood
of Adam with all the mischief
and feebleness that followed.
For in all this our good lord
showed his own son and Adam
but one man.
The power [*healing power*] and the
    goodness that we have is of Jesus
Christ, the feebleness and blindness
that we have is of Adam,
which two were shown in the servant.
And thus has our good lord Jesu taken upon him all our blame;
and therefore our father
may not will more blame representative [*assigned*]—
to us than to his own beloved son Jesu Christ.
Thus was he the servant before his
coming in the earth being the case [*standing*]
ready before the father in
purpose till what time

he would send him to do the reverent
deed by which mankind was brought
again to heaven.
That is to say, notwithstanding that he is god,
equal with the father as regards the godhead,
but in his foreseeing purpose, that he would be man
to save man
in fulfilling of the will; of his father, so
he stood before his father
as a servant,
wilfully taking upon him all our load [*freight* or *cargo* or *heavy
    burden*].
And then he departs full ready
at the father's will,
and immediately he fell full praise
into the maiden's womb,
having no regard to himself or to his hard pains.
The white tunic is his flesh; the being
of one piece [*singleness*]
is that there was exactly nothing between—the godhead and
    the manhood.
The straightness [*tight fit*],
is poverty, the age is of Adam's labour [*making*].
The defacing [*lacking* or *defection in use*] is the seat of
Adam's labour. The shortness shows
the servant labour.
And thus I saw the son standing saying in his reason:
["] Lo, my dear
father, I stand before thee in Adam's tunic all ready to
depart and to run.
I would be in the earth to thy worthiness
when it is thy will to send me. ["]
How long shall I desire it?
Full truly wise the son
when it was the father's will,
and how long
he should

desire, that is to say a call by name the godhead,
for he is the wisdom of the father.
Wherefore this reason was shown
in understanding of the manhood of Christ's.
For all mankind that shall be saved by the sweet incarnation
and passion
of Christ,—all is the manhood of Christ.
For he is head, and we but
his members,
to which members this day
and the time in unknown
when every passing woe and sorrow shall have an end and the
everlasting joy and bliss [*happiness*]
shall be fulfilled,
which day and time for to see,
all the company of heaven longs or desires.
And all that be under heaven,
which shall come thither
their way is by longing and deserving;
which deserving and longing was shown in the servant
being the case [*standing*] before the lord
otherwise in the son being the case [*standing*] before the father
in Adam's tunic.
For the longing and desire of all
mankind that shall be saved
appeared in Jesu.
For Jesus is in all that shall be saved,
and all that shall be saved is in Jesu,
And all of the benevolence of god with obedience,
meekness, patience and
virtue that longs to us.
Also in this marvellous example I have—
teaching within me,
as it were the beginning of an A B C,
whereby I may have some understanding of all our lord's
reason,
for the secrets of the revelation

be hid therein notwithstanding that all the [*each*]
showing is full of secrets.
The sitting of the father betokens [*is a sign*]
of godhead, that is to say for showing
of rest and peace [*silence*],
for in the godhead there can be no labour
and that he shows himself as lord betokens
[*is a sign*] of our manhood.
The standing of the servant betokens [*is a sign*] labour
and on the left side betokens [*is a sign*]
that he was not worthy to stand equal exactly before the lord.
His departure was the godhead,
the running was the manhood;
for the godhead departs [*starts*] from
the father into the maiden's womb,
falling into the taking of our nature,
and in this falling he took great agonizing
The agonizing that he took
was our flesh, in which as soon as,
he had feeling of deadly pains.
By that—he stood dreadful [*to be awed*] before the lord
and not equal exactly betoken [*is a sign*] that
his disguise [*clothing*] was not honest [*appropriate*] to stand
equal exactly before the lord,
not that it might not,
nor should it not be his office
while he was a labourer;
nor also he might not sit with the lord
in rest and peace [*silence*] till he had
won his portion rightfully with
his hard work;
and by his left side, that the
father left his own son wilfully in
the manhood to suffer all
man's pain without sparing him.
By that his tunic was at the point to be ragged and rent is
    understood

the crosses [*assaults*],
and the scourges,
the thorns, and the nails,
the drawing and the dragging
his tender flesh renting—as I saw in
some a part.
The flesh was rent from the head
pain,
falling in pieces unto the time
the bleeding stopped; and than
it began to dry again, cleaving to the bone.
And by the rolling [*tossing about*] and twisting,
groaning and
moaning, is understood that he might never rise all mightily
          [*powerfully*]
from that time that he was falling into the maiden's womb,
till his body was slain and dead,
he yielding the soul to the
father's hand with all mankind for
whom he was sent.
At this point he began first to
show his power,
for there he went into hell,
and when he was there then he
raised up the great root [*mass*] out of the deep [*depths*],
which rightfully was
bound to him high heaven. The body lay in the grave till
Easter morning;
and from that time he lay never more.
For there was rightly ended the rolling [*tossing about*]
and the twisting,
the groaning
the moaning;
and our stinking deadly flesh, that god's son took upon him
          which was Adam's old tunic depart,
bare and short,
then by our saviour was

made fair, new, white and bright,
and of endless cleanness wide and flowing,
fair and rich [the sense of being—*powerful*] than was
the disguise [*clothing*] which saw the father.
For that disguise [*clothing*] was blue, and
Christ's disguise [*clothing*] is now of fair familiar mixture
which is so marvellous that I can not describe,
for it is all of very reverence.
Now seated the lord not on earth wilderness, but he sits
on his rich and noble seat,
which he made in heaven most to his liking.
Now being the case [*stands*] not the son before the father as a
     servant before the lord, feebly disguised [*clothed*]
in manner naked,
but he stands before the father equal exactly
richly disguised [*clothed*] in blissful [*happiness*] largely
[*liberally*] with a crown upon his head of precious abundance.
For it was shown that we be his crown [*discoursing of wisdom/*
     discretion/perfection of virtue],
which crown [*discoursing of wisdom/discretion/perfection of*
virtue] is the father's joy, the son's reverence, the holy
ghost's liking,
and endless astonishing bliss [*happiness*] to all that be in
     heaven.
Now being the case [*stands*] not the son before the father
on the left side as a labourer,
but he sits on the father's right hand
in endless rest and peace [*silence*].
But it is not meant that the son sits on the right hand beside,
as one man sits by another in this life,
for there is no such sitting,
as to my sight,
in the trinity;
but he sits on his father's right hand, that is to say exactly in
the highest nobility of the father's joy.
Now is the—wife [*spouse*],
god's son,

in peace [*silence*] with his loved wife,
which is the first maiden of endless joy.
Now sits the son,
true god and true man,
in his walled city in rest and peace [*silence*], which his father
      has dished [*prepared*] to him
of endless purpose, and the father in the son,
and the holy ghost in the father and in the son.

Bibliography

Bernard of Clairvaux. *On the Song of Songs,* vols. ii–iv. Trans. Irene Edmunds. Kalamazoo, Michigan: Cistercian Publications, 1980.

Bradley, Ritamary. *Julian's Way.* London: Harper Collins Religious, 1992.

Bynum, Caroline Walker. *Jesus as Mother.* Berkeley: University of California Press, 1982.

Colledge, Edmund, and Walsh, James, editors. *A Book of Showings to the Anchoress of Julian of Norwich,* vol. 1–11. Toronto: Pontifical Institute of Mediaeval Studies, 1978.

Cooper, Austin. *Julian of Norwich.* Mystic, Connecticut: Twenty-third Publications, 1986.

Durka, Gloria. *Praying with Julian of Norwich.* Winona, Minnesota: St. Mary's Press, Christian Brothers Publications, 1989.

Fiorenza, Elisabeth Schussler. *Bread Not Stone.* Boston: Beacon Press, 1984.

Fiorenza, Elisabeth Schussler. *In Memory of Her.* New York: Crossroad Publishing Company, 1983.

Gilligan, Carol. *In a Different Voice.* Cambridge: Harvard University Press, 1982.

Jantzen, Grace. *Julian of Norwich.* New York: Paulist Press, 1988.

Johnson, Elizabeth A. *She Who Is.* New York: Crossroad Publishing Company, 1992.

99

McHaffie, Barbara. *Her Story*. Philadelphia: Fortress Press, 1986.

Pelphrey, Brant. *Christ Our Mother: Julian of Norwich*. Wilmington, Delaware: Michael Glazier, Inc., 1989.

Upjohn, Sheila. *In Search of Julian of Norwich*. London: Darton, Longman and Todd, Ltd., 1989.

Other Readings

Bonhoffer, Dietrich. *Meditating on the Word.* Trans. David McI. Gracie. Cambridge: Cowley Publications, 1986.

Brum, Emilie, and Epinery-Burgard, Georgette. *Women Mystics in Medieval Europe.* Translated by Sheila Hughes. New York: Paragon House, 1989.

Carey, George. *Why I Believe in a Personal God.* Wheaton, Illinois: Harold Shaw Publications, 1989.

Daly, Mary. *Beyond God the Father.* Boston: Beacon Press, 1973.

Durant, William. *The Story of Civilization: The Age of Faith,* vol. iv. New York: Simon and Schuster, 1950.

Fiorenza, Elisabeth Schussler. *But She Said.* Boston: Beacon Press, 1992.

Grey, Mary. *Feminism, Redemption and the Christian Tradition.* Mystic, Connecticut: Twenty-Third Publications, 1990.

Kreeft, Peter. *The Unaborted Socrates.* Downers Grove, Illinois: Intervarsity Press, 1983.

Labarge, Margaret Wade. *A Small Sound of the Trumpet: Women in Medieval Life.* London: A Hamish Hamilton Paperback, 1986.

Leddy, Mary Jo; De Roo, Remi; and Roche, Douglas. *In the Eye of the Catholic Storm: The Church Since Vatican II.* Toronto: Harper Perennial Press, 1992.

O'Connor, Kathleen. *The Wisdom Literature*. Wilmington, Delaware: Michael Glazier, 1988.

Oesterley, W. O. E., and Robinson, T. H. *Introduction to the Books of the Old Testament*. London: S. P. C. K., 1955.

Robinson, H. Wheeler. *Inspiration and Revelation in the Old Testament*. Oxford: Clarendon Press, 1956.

Spong, J. S. *Born of a Woman*. San Francisco: Harper, 1992.

Stone, Merlin. *When God Was a Woman*. New York: Dorset Press, 1976.

Suenens, Leon-Joseph. *Your God?* London: Darton, Longman and Todd, 1978.

von Rad, Gerhard. *Wisdom in Israel*. Translated by James Martin. London: SCM Press, 1970.

Wakeman, Henry. *History of the Church of England*. London: Rivington, 1955.

Wilson, Katherine, editor. *Medieval Women Writers*. Athens: University of Georgia Press, 1984.